Puerto Princesa Pictorial

Puerto Princesa Pictorial

Rob Benton

Esotericom®

All photographs by Rob Benton

ISBN 978-0-9980682-4-4

"For here we have no lasting city,
but we seek the city which is to come."

Hebrews 13:14

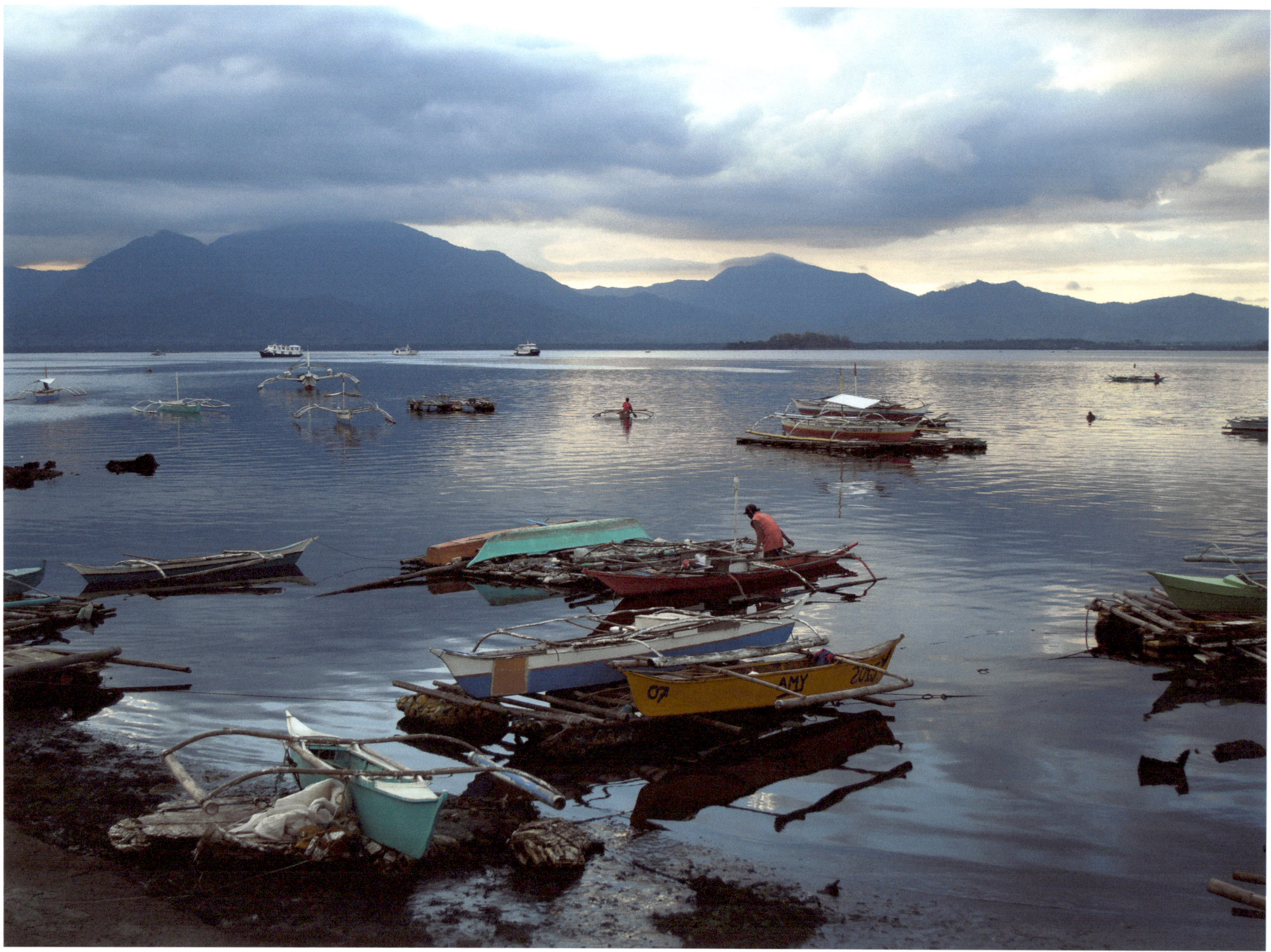
07
AMY

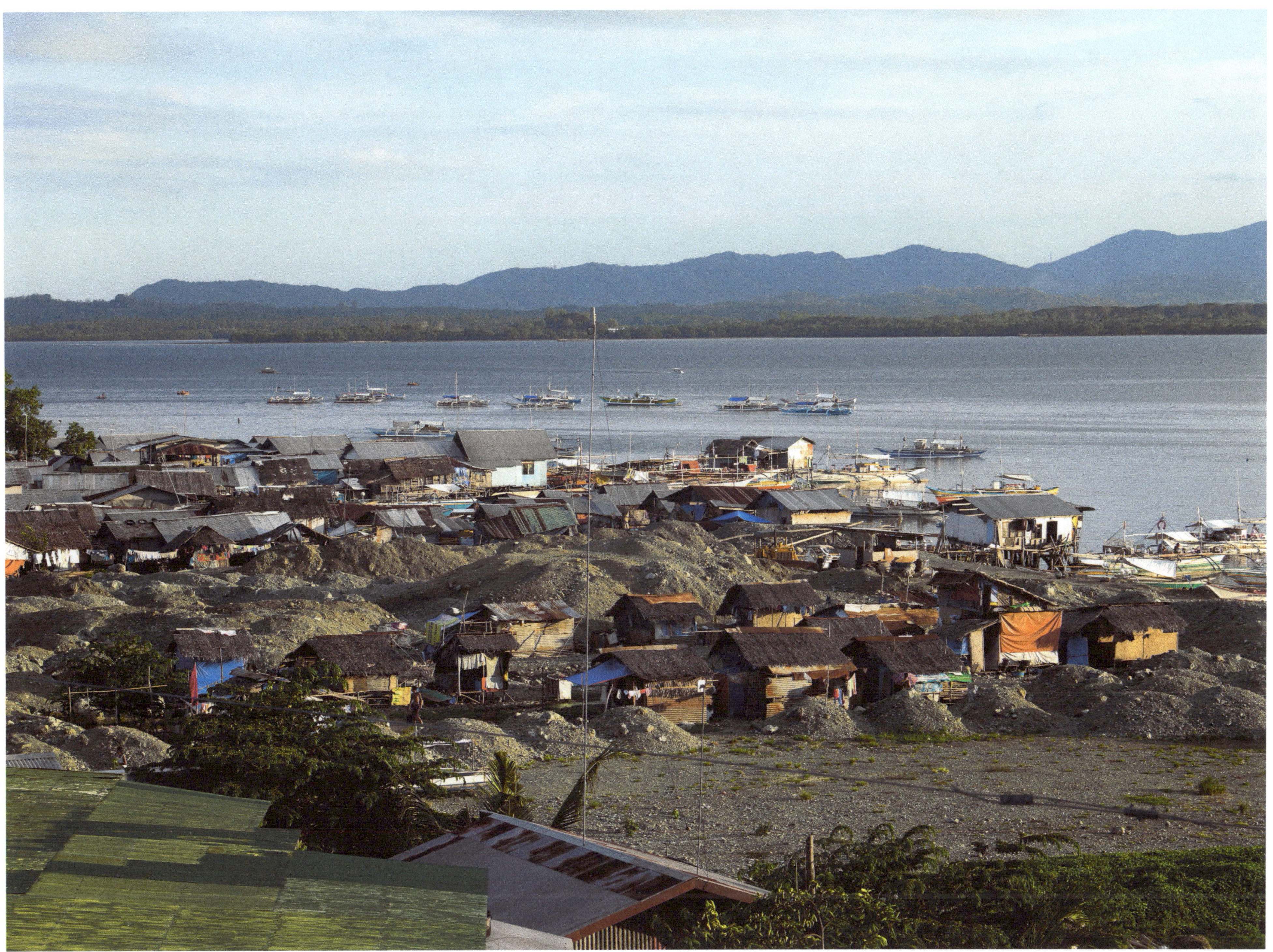

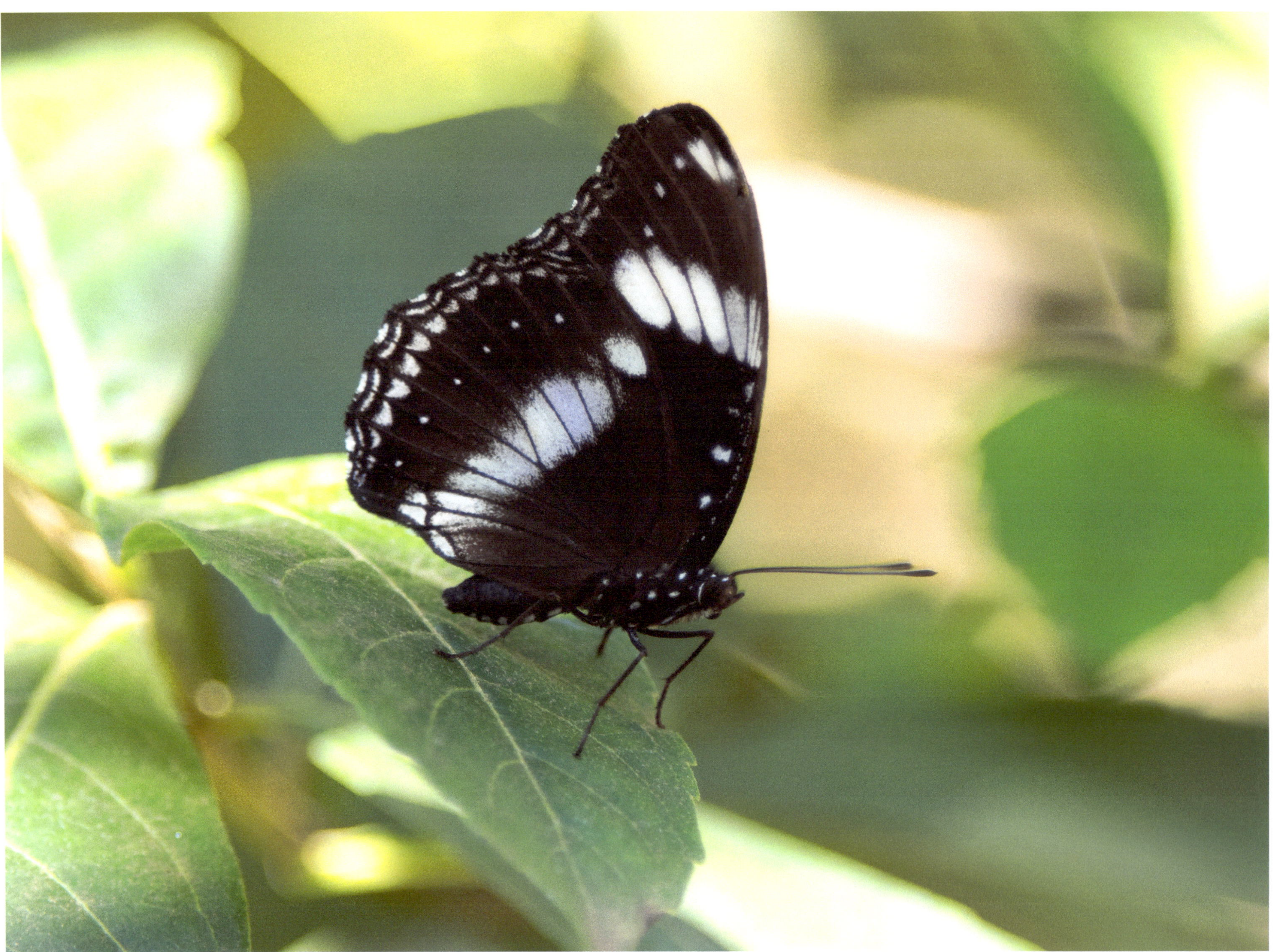

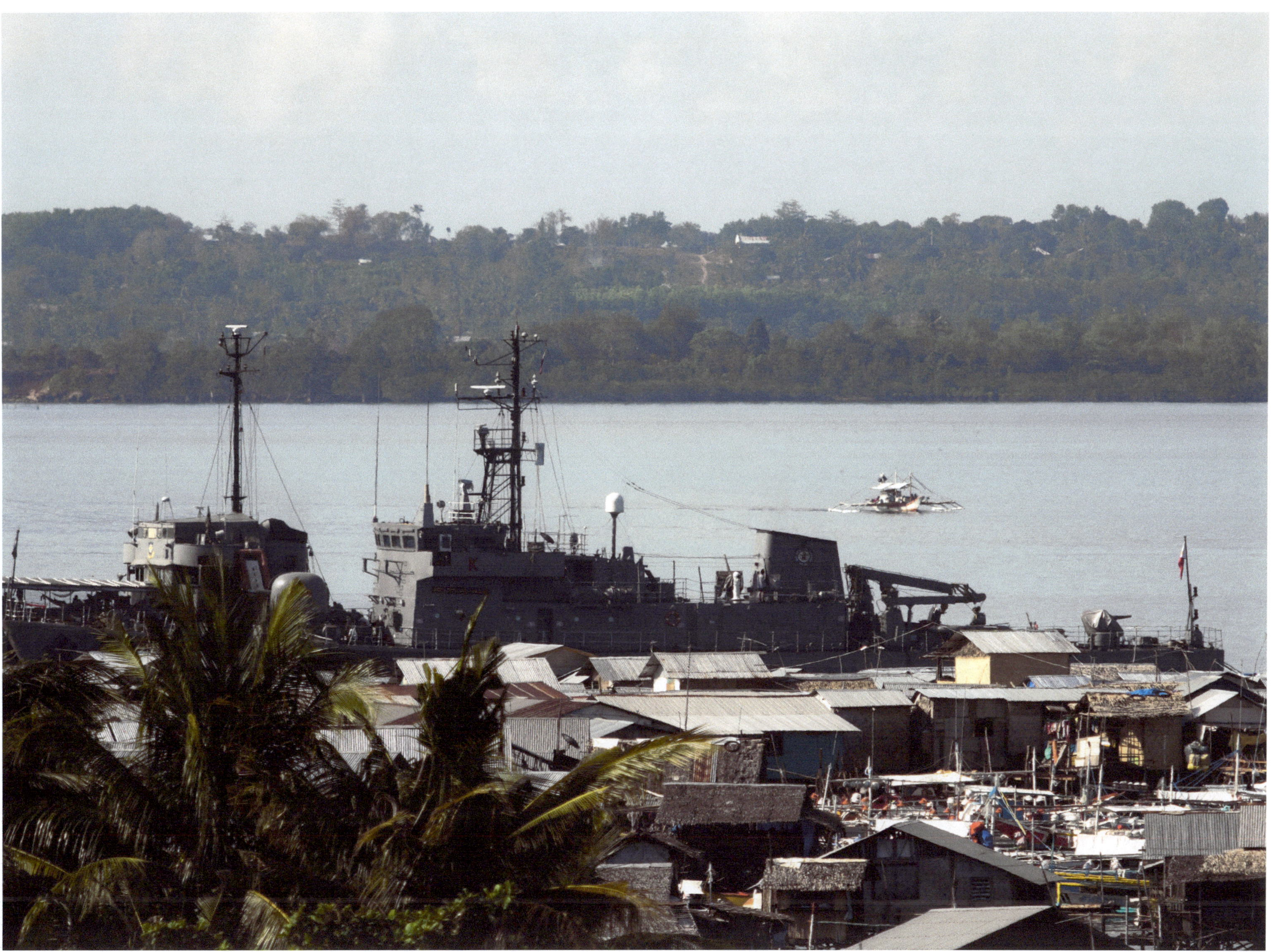

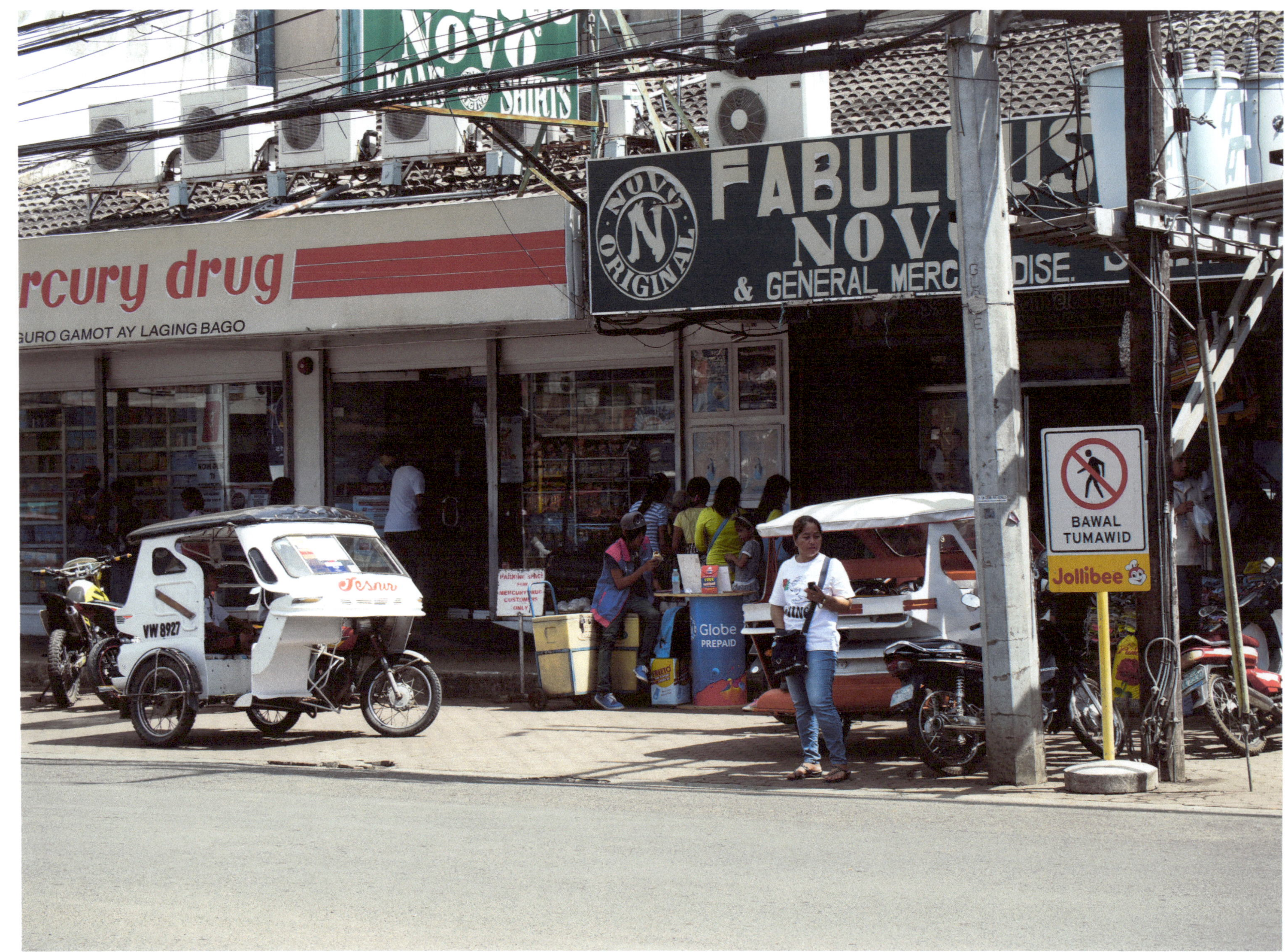

NOVO
SHIRTS
rcury drug
GURO GAMOT AY LAGING BAGO
NOVO ORIGINAL
FABUL
US
NOVO
& GENERAL MERC
DISE.
VW 8927
Globe
PREPAID
BAWAL
TUMAWID
Jollibee

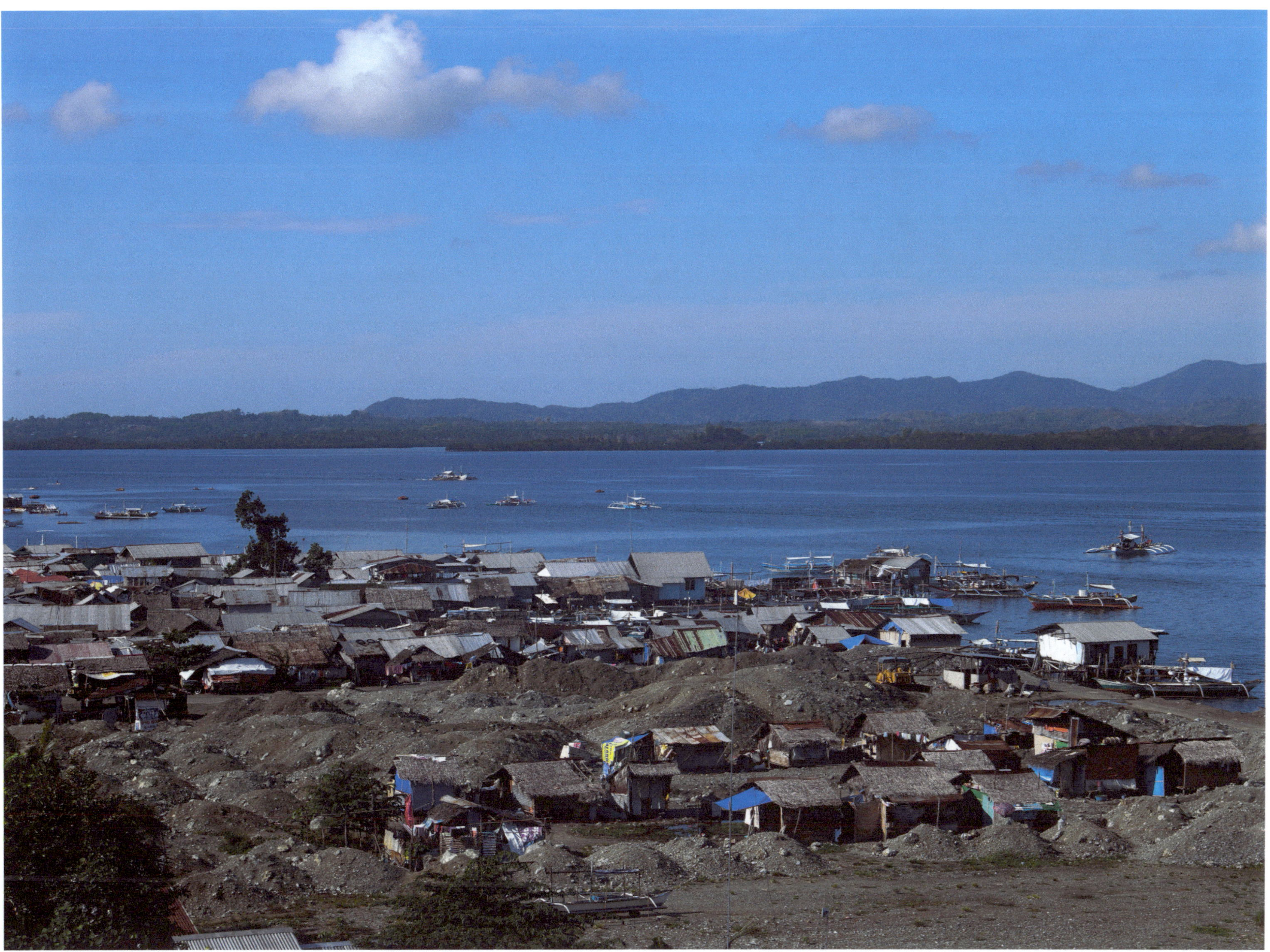

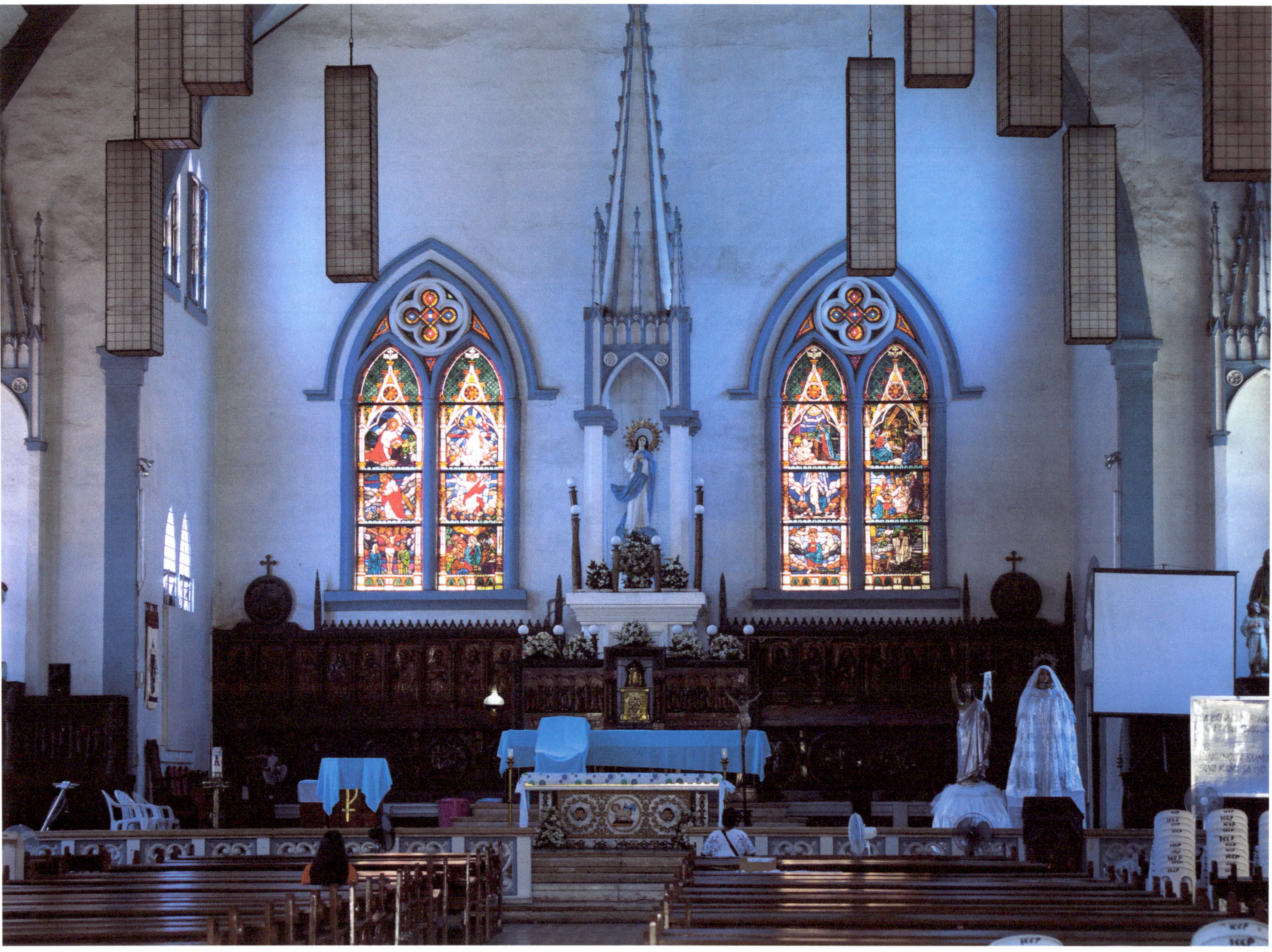

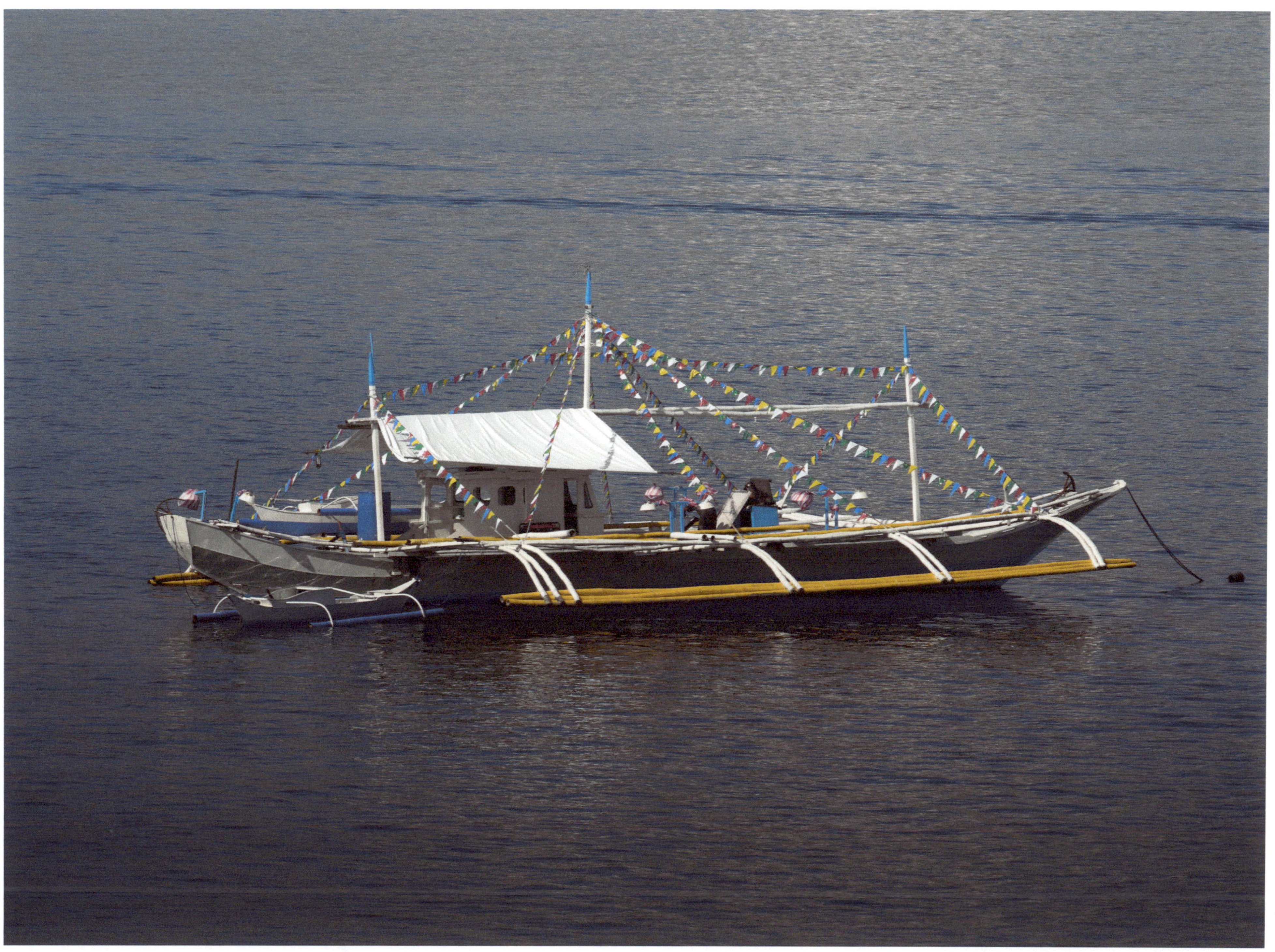

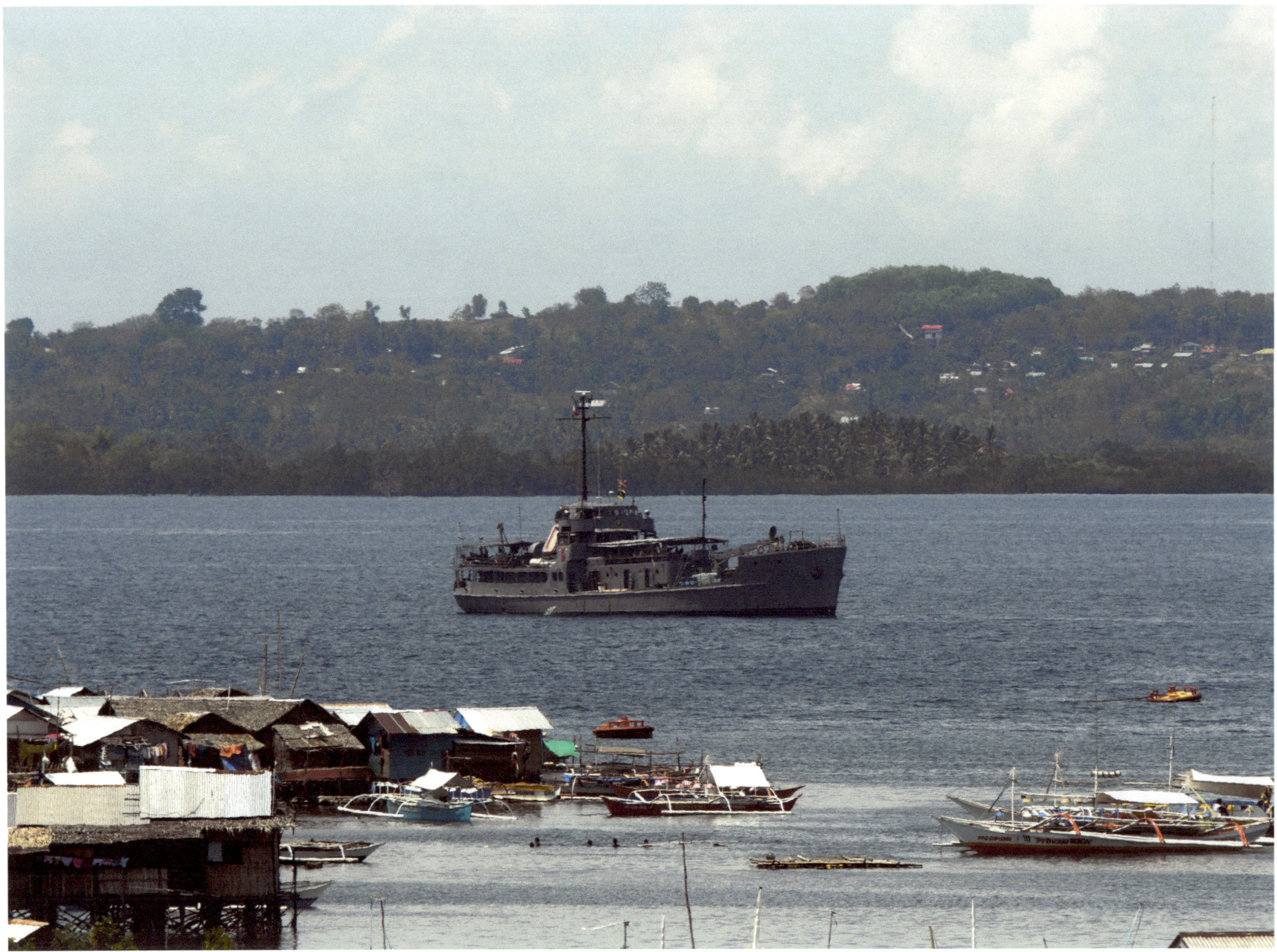

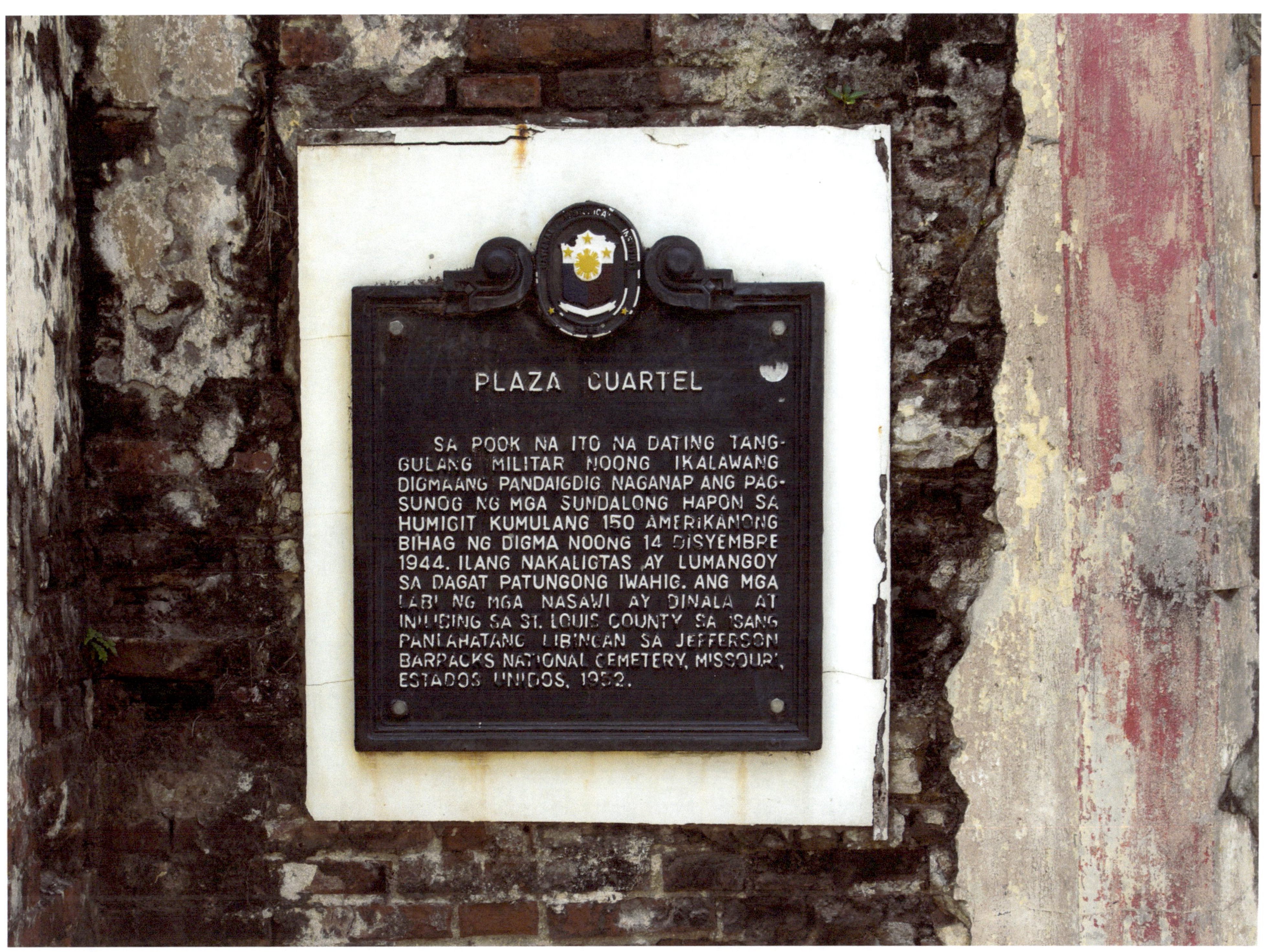
PLAZA CUARTEL
SA POOK NA ITO NA DATING TANG-
GULANG MILITAR NOONG IKALAWANG
DIGMAANG PANDAIGDIG NAGANAP ANG PAG-
SUNOG NG MGA SUNDALONG HAPON SA
HUMIGIT KUMULANG 150 AMERIKANONG
BIHAG NG DIGMA NOONG 14 DISYEMBRE
1944. ILANG NAKALIGTAS AY LUMANGOY
SA DAGAT PATUNGONG IWAHIG. ANG MGA
LABI NG MGA NASAWI AY DINALA AT
INILIBING SA ST. LOUIS COUNTY SA ISANG
PANLAHATANG LIBINGAN SA JEFFERSON
BARRACKS NATIONAL CEMETERY, MISSOURI,
ESTADOS UNIDOS, 1952.

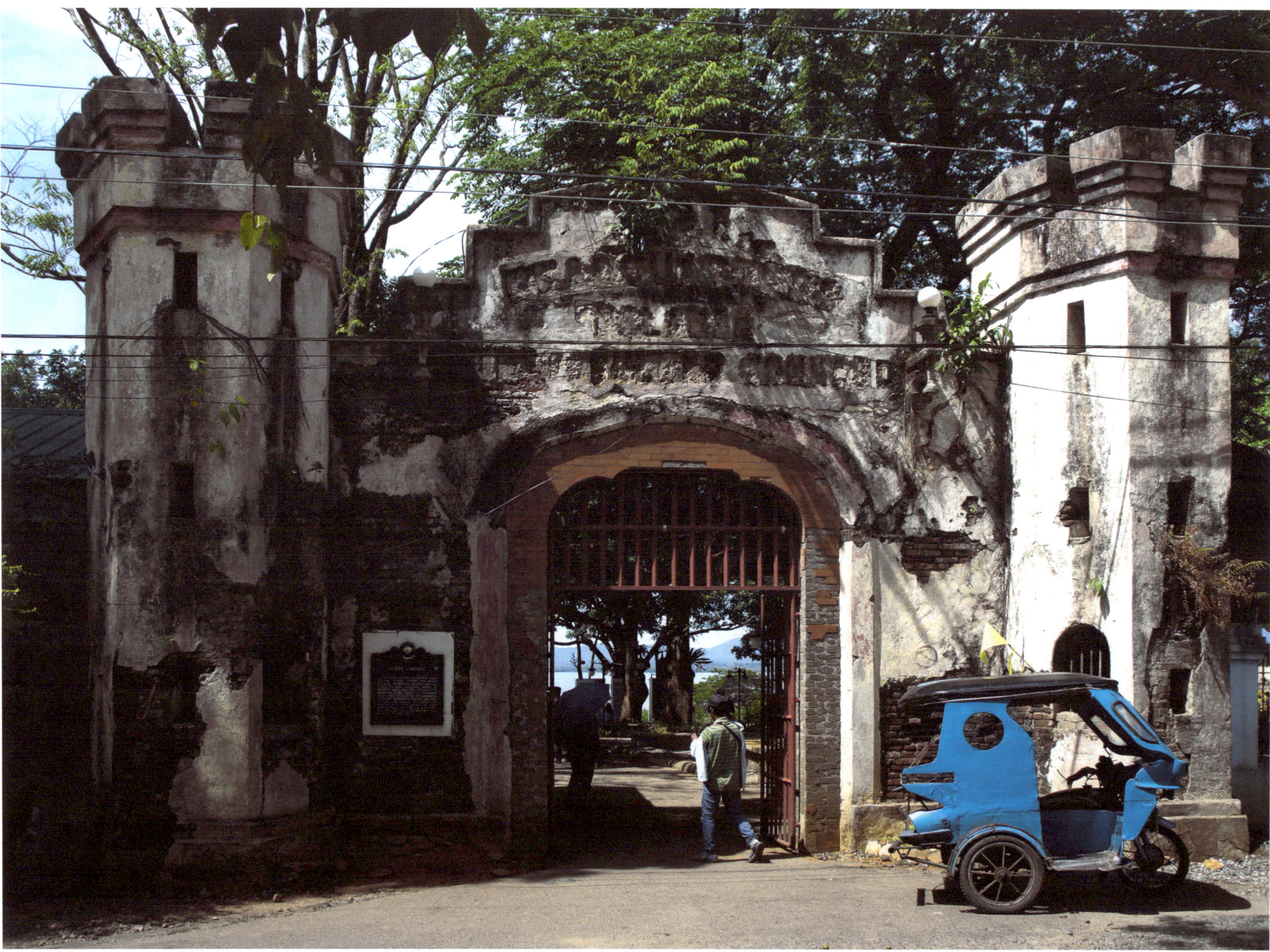

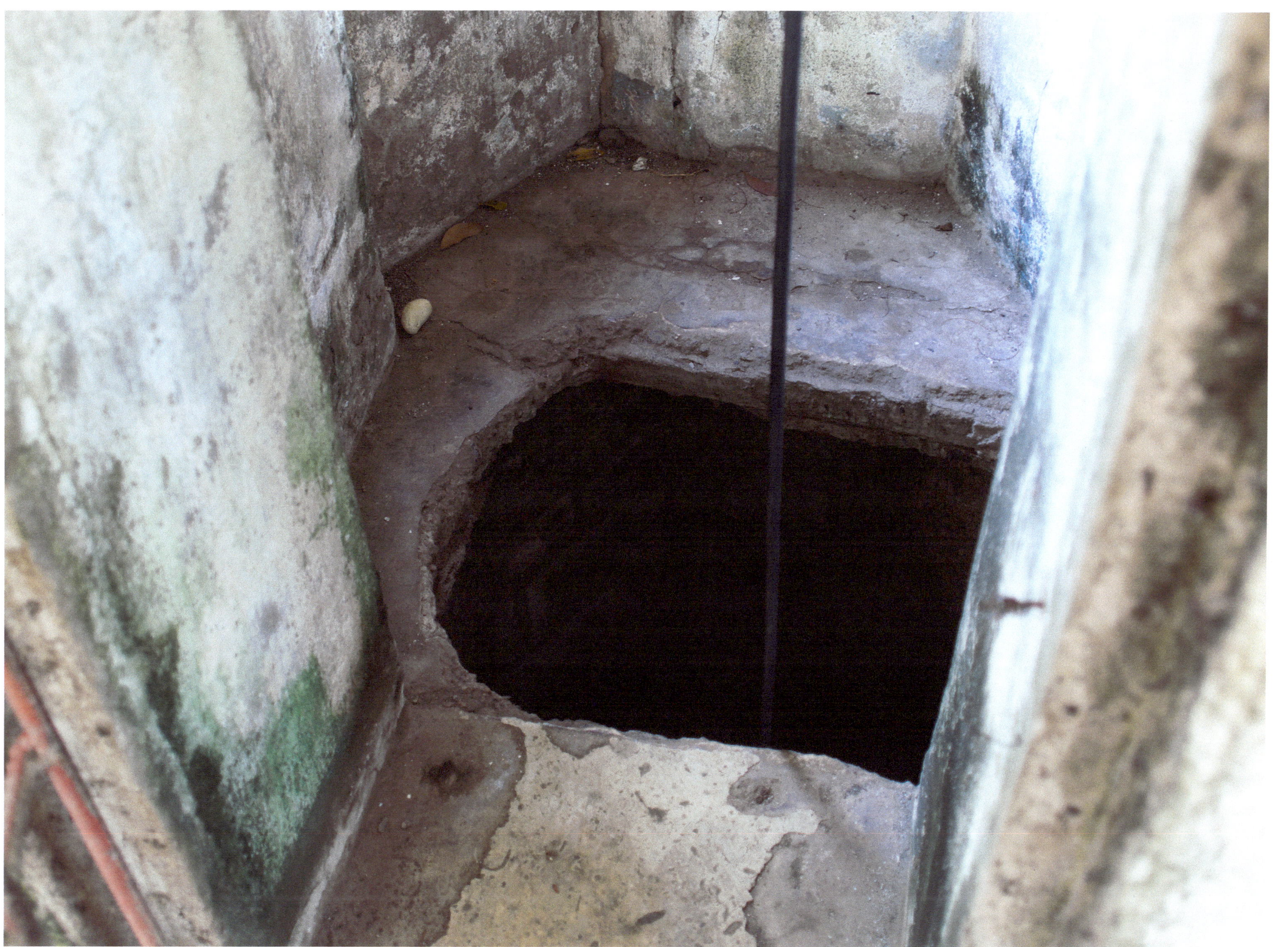

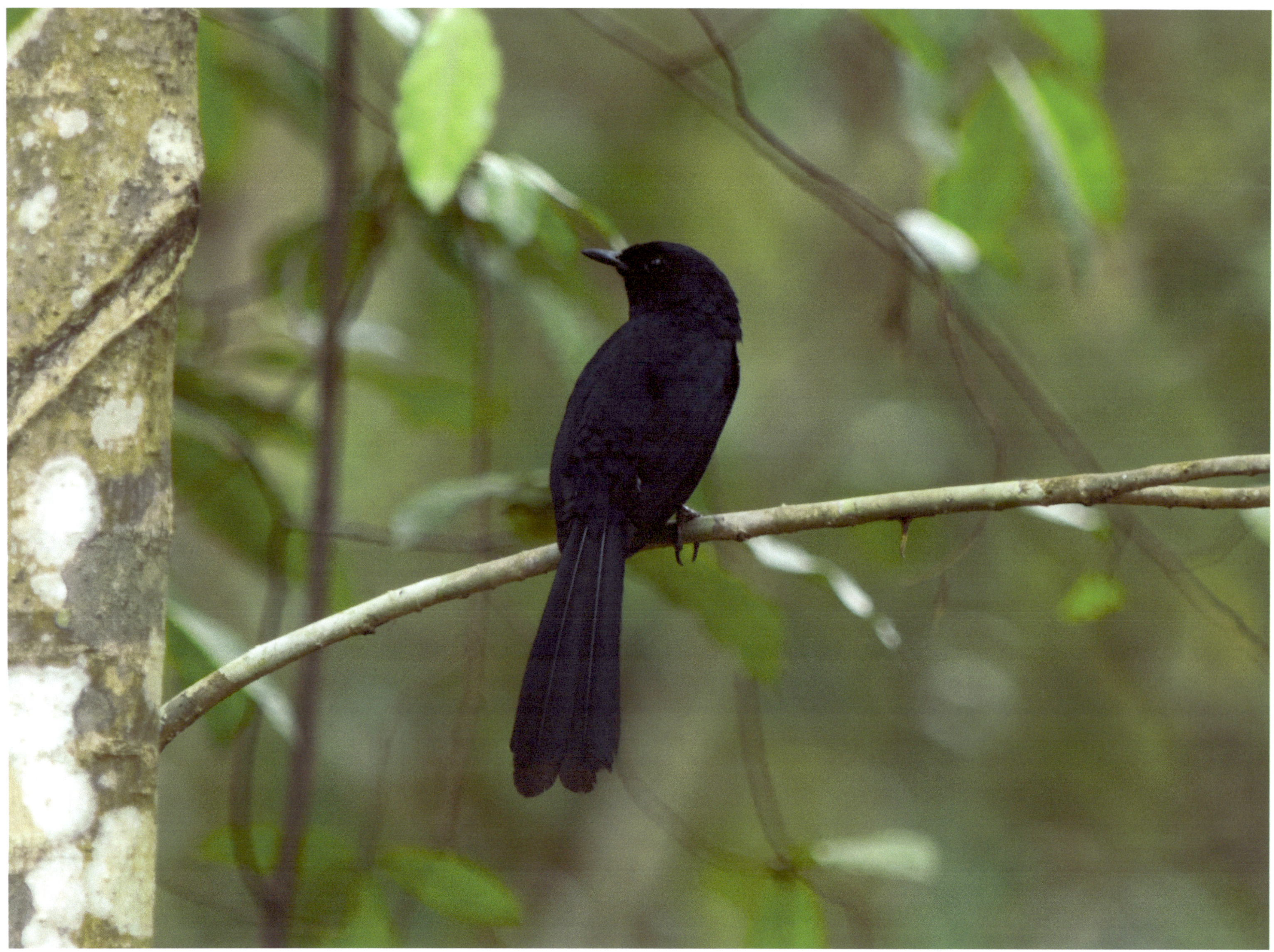

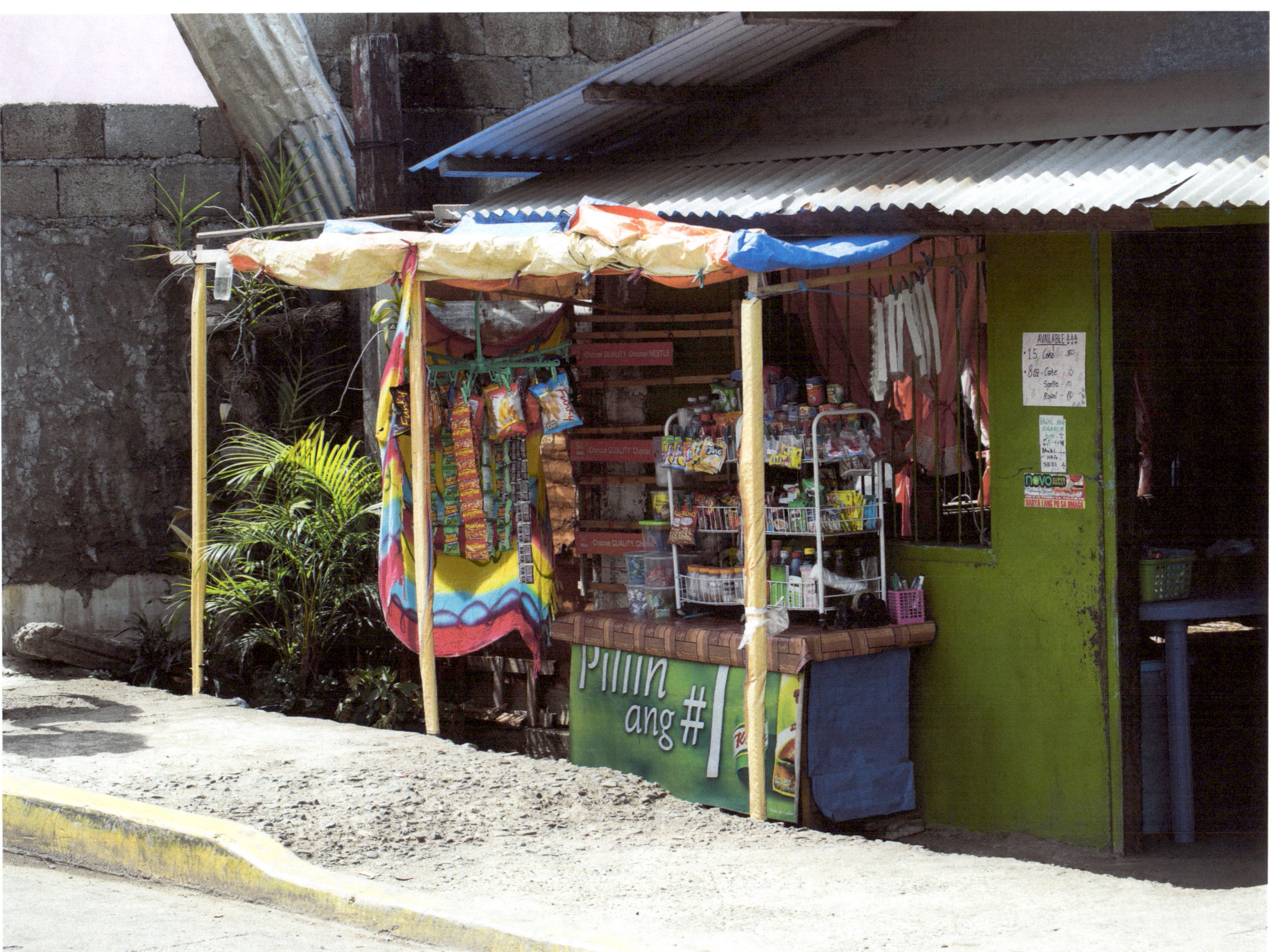
Choose QUALITY Choose NESTLE
Choose QUALITY Choose
Choose QUALITY
AVAILABLE
1.5 Coke 50
8oz Coke 10
Sprite 10
Royal 10
novo SUPER MARKET
BARYA LANG PO SA UMAGA
Piliin
ang #1

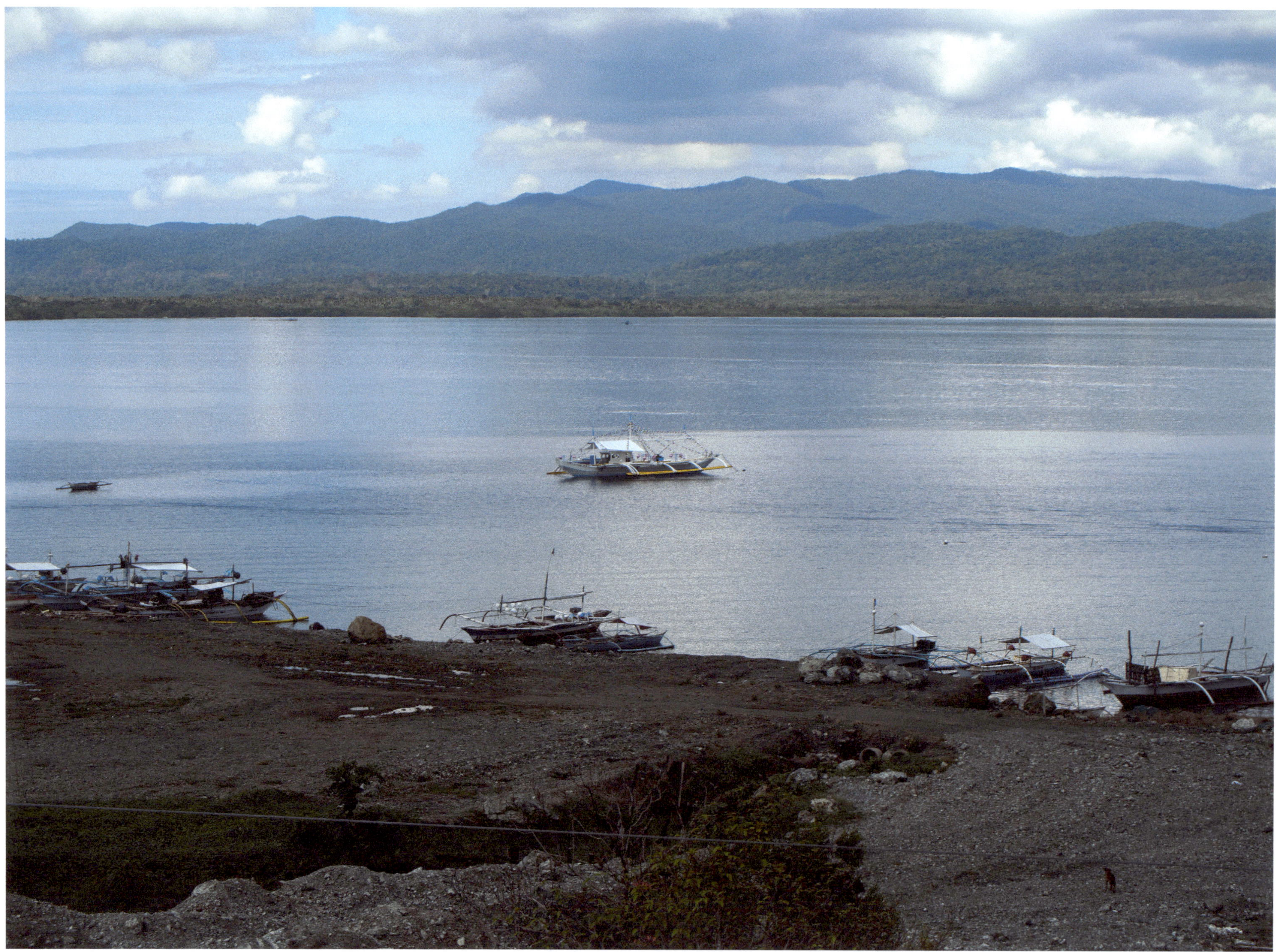

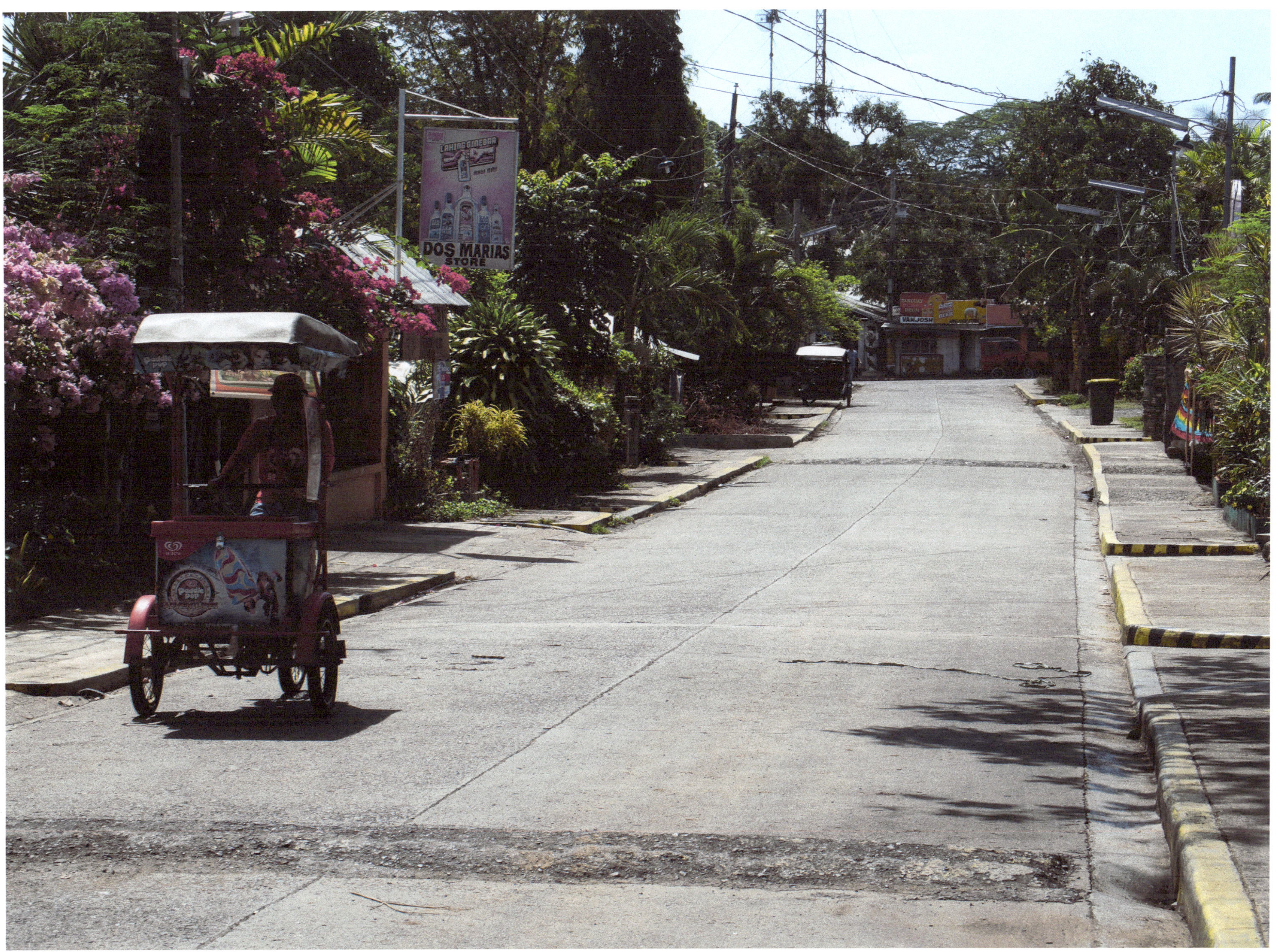
LAHING GINEBRA
DOS MARIAS
STORE
VANJOSH
BEER

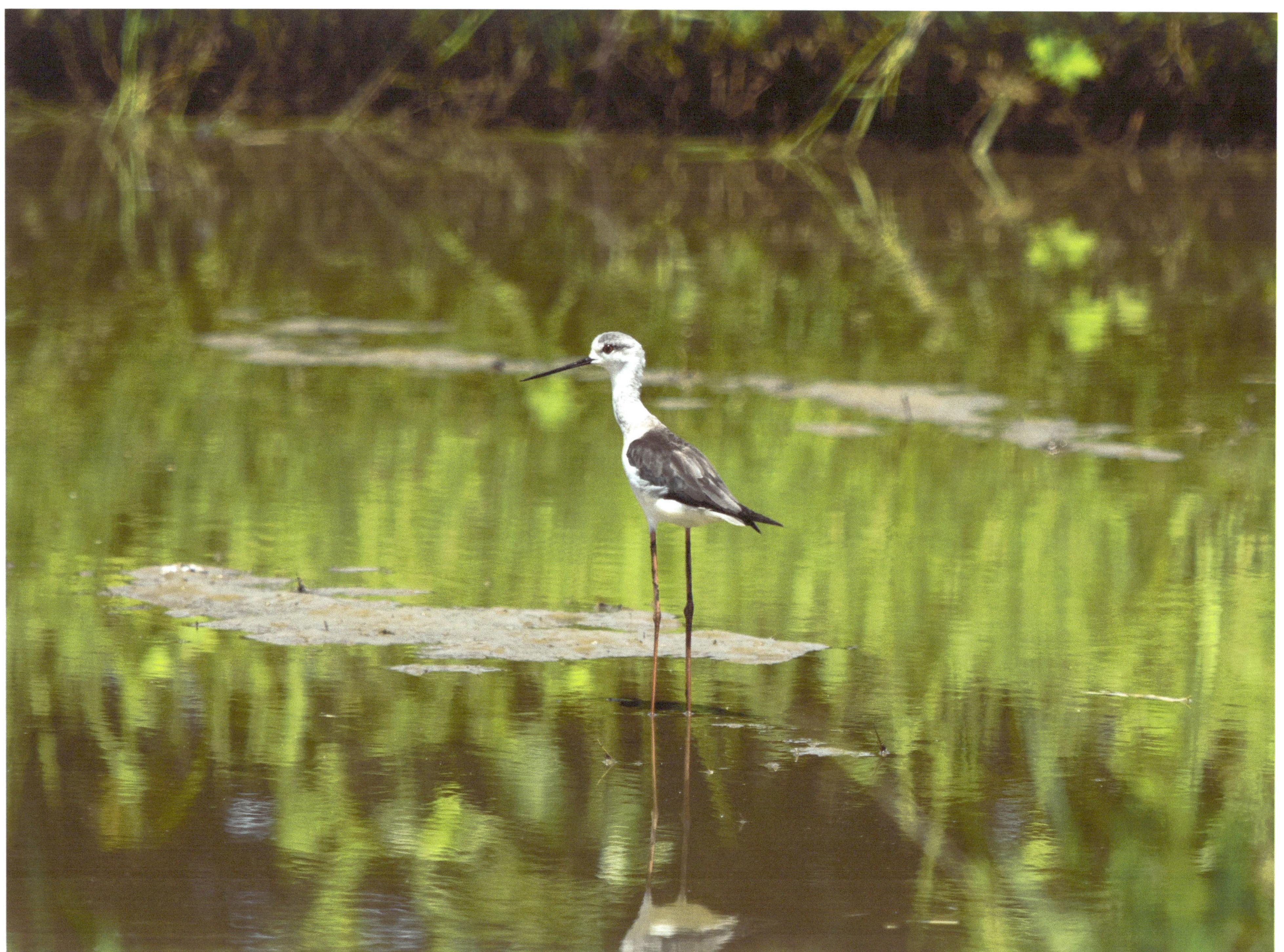

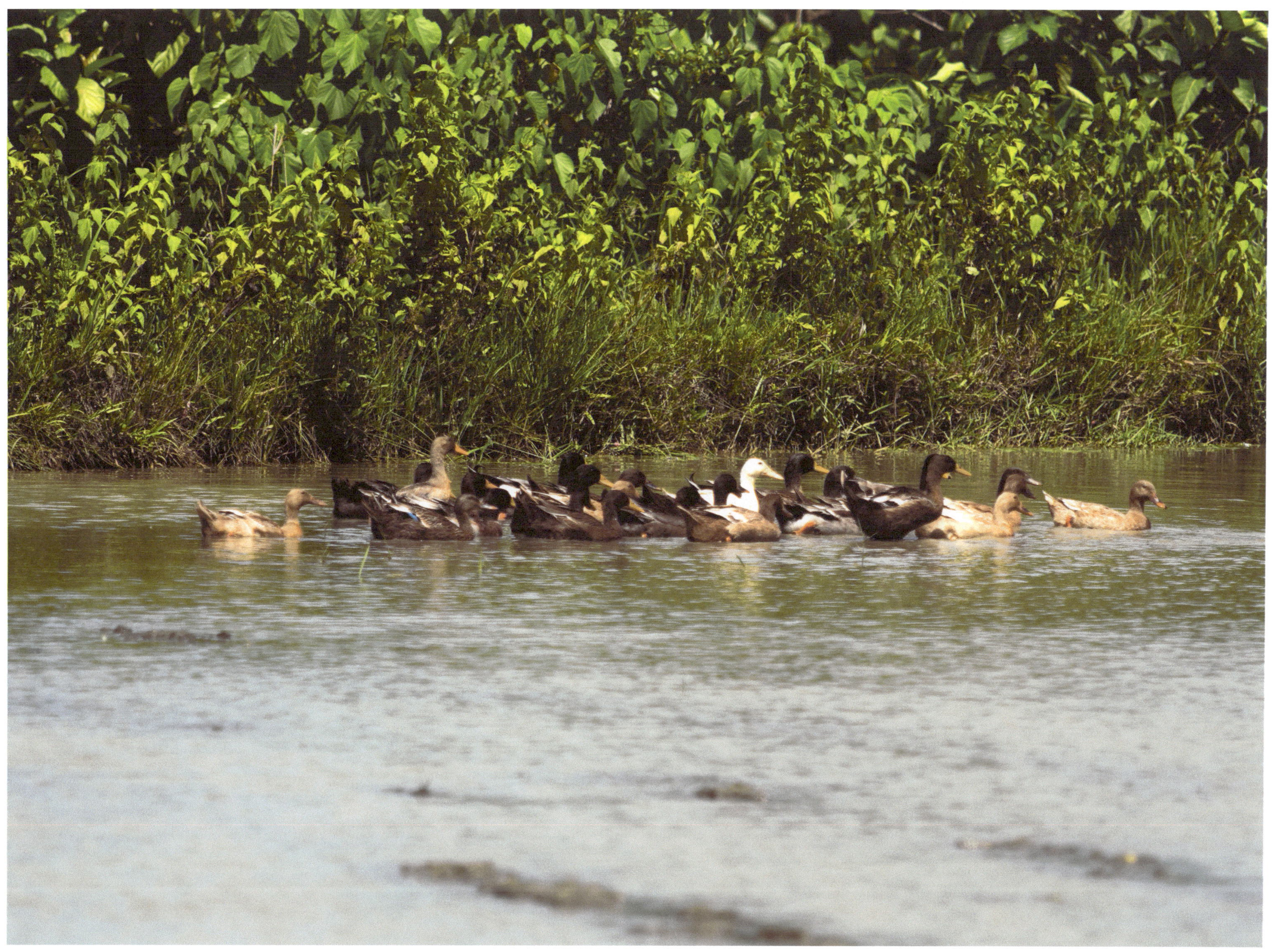

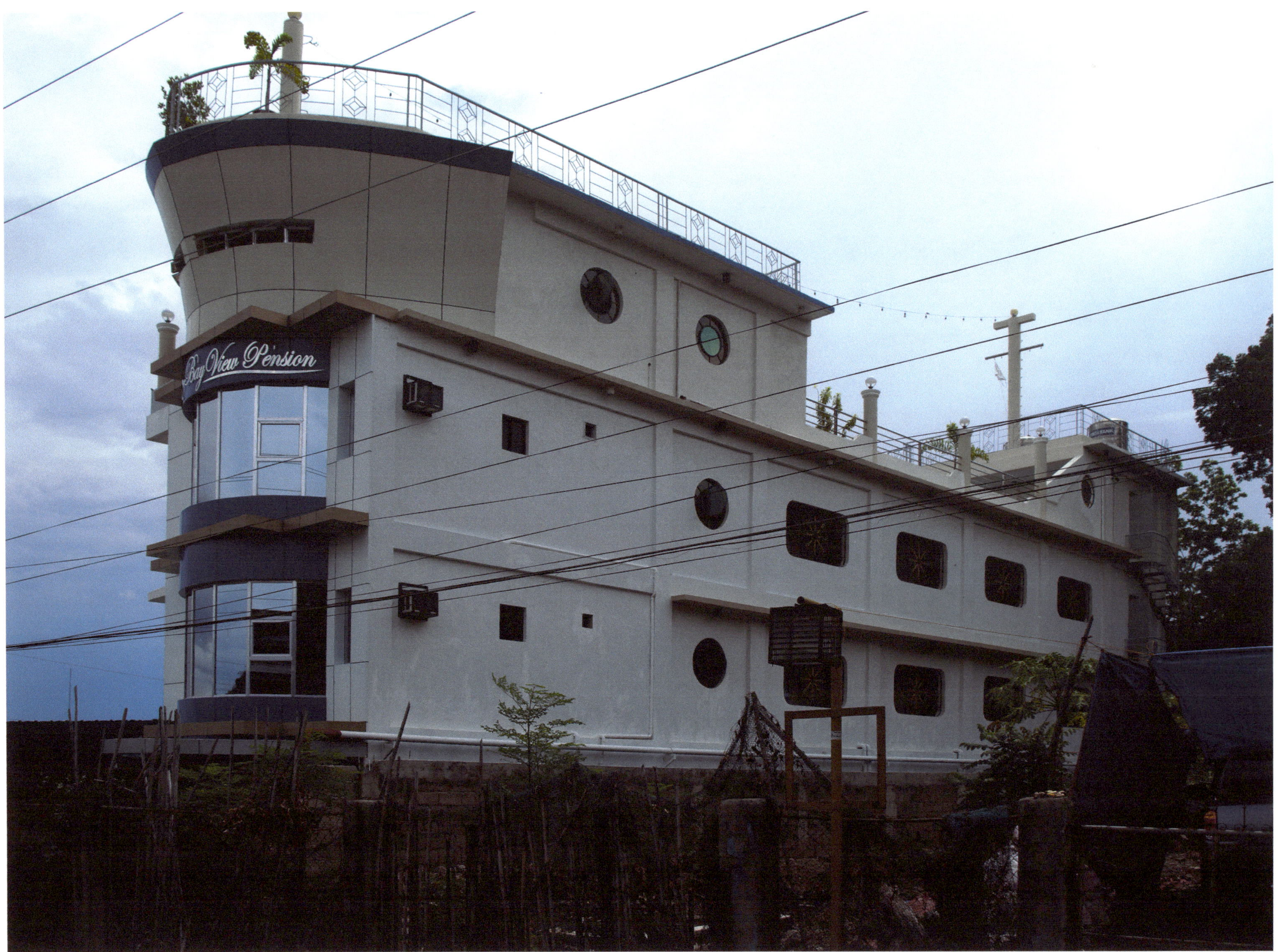
Bay View Pension

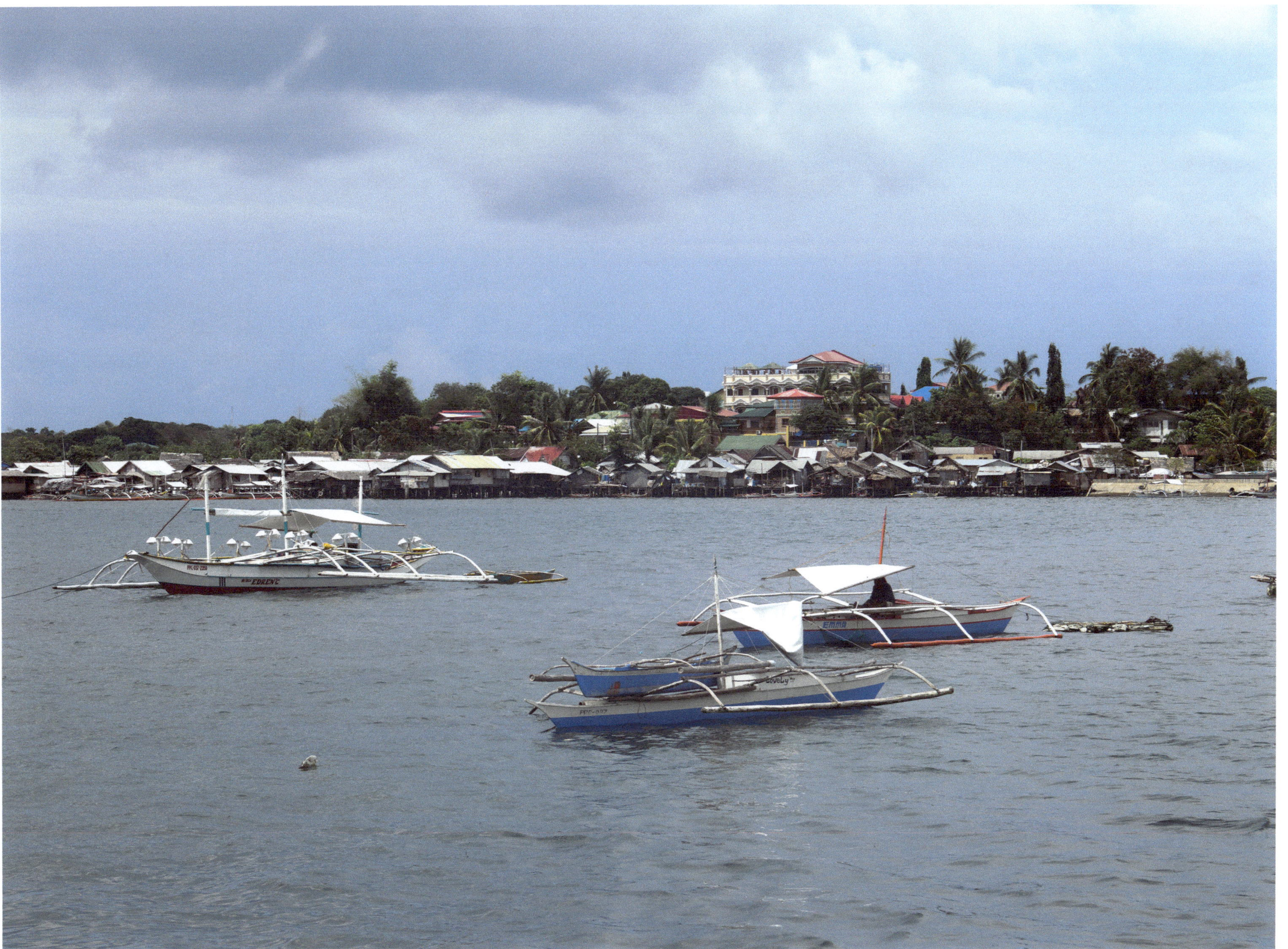

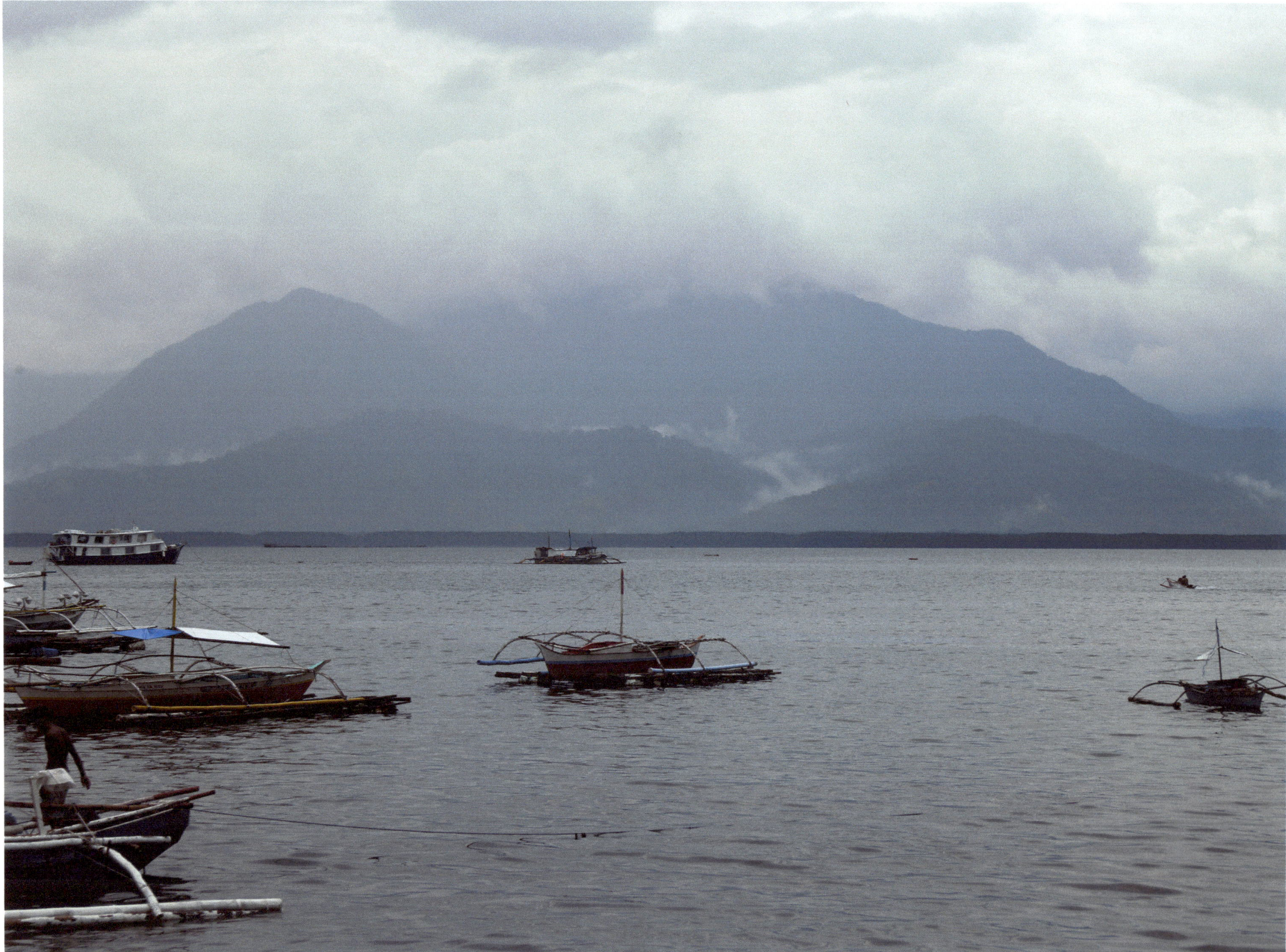

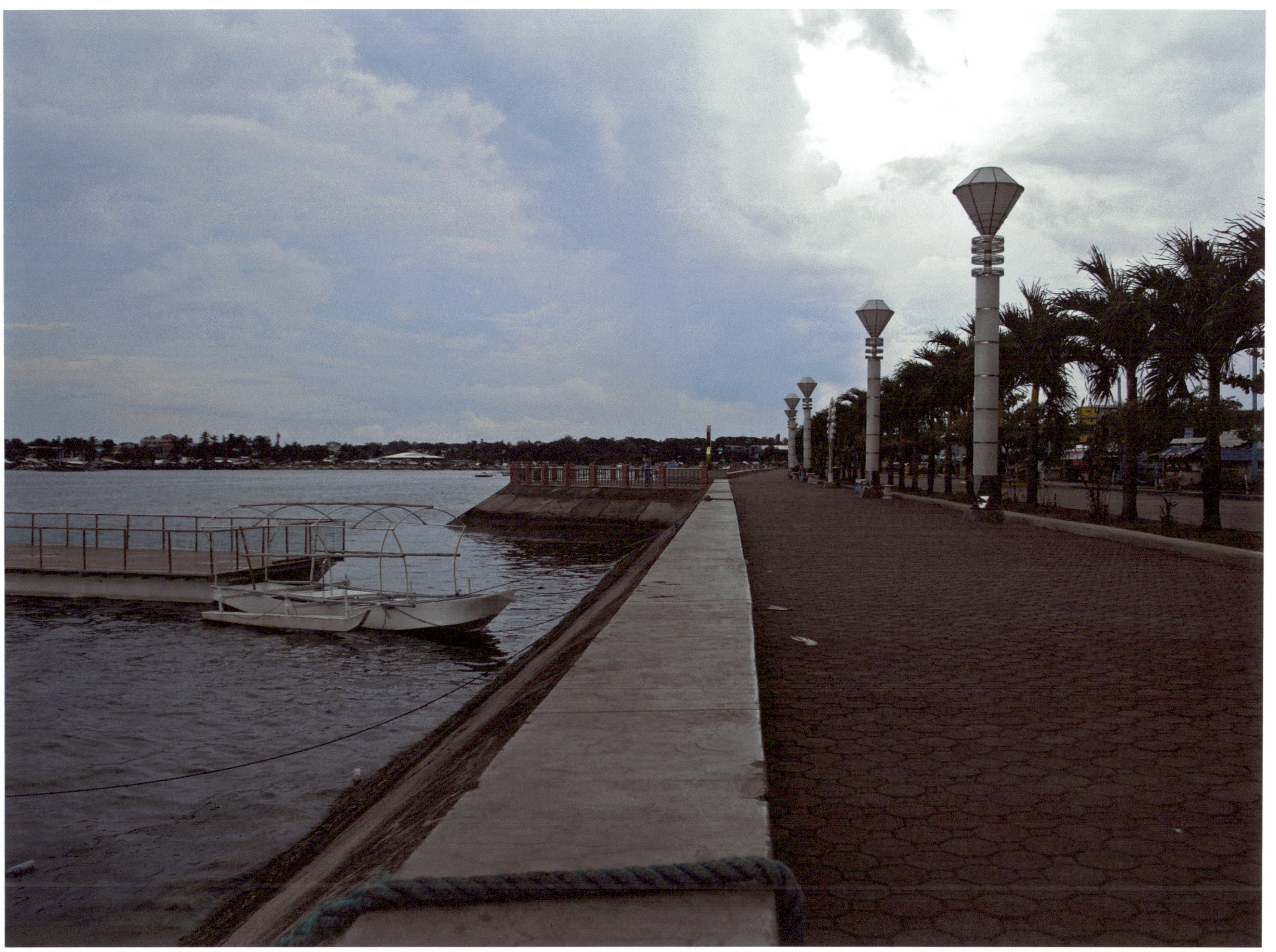

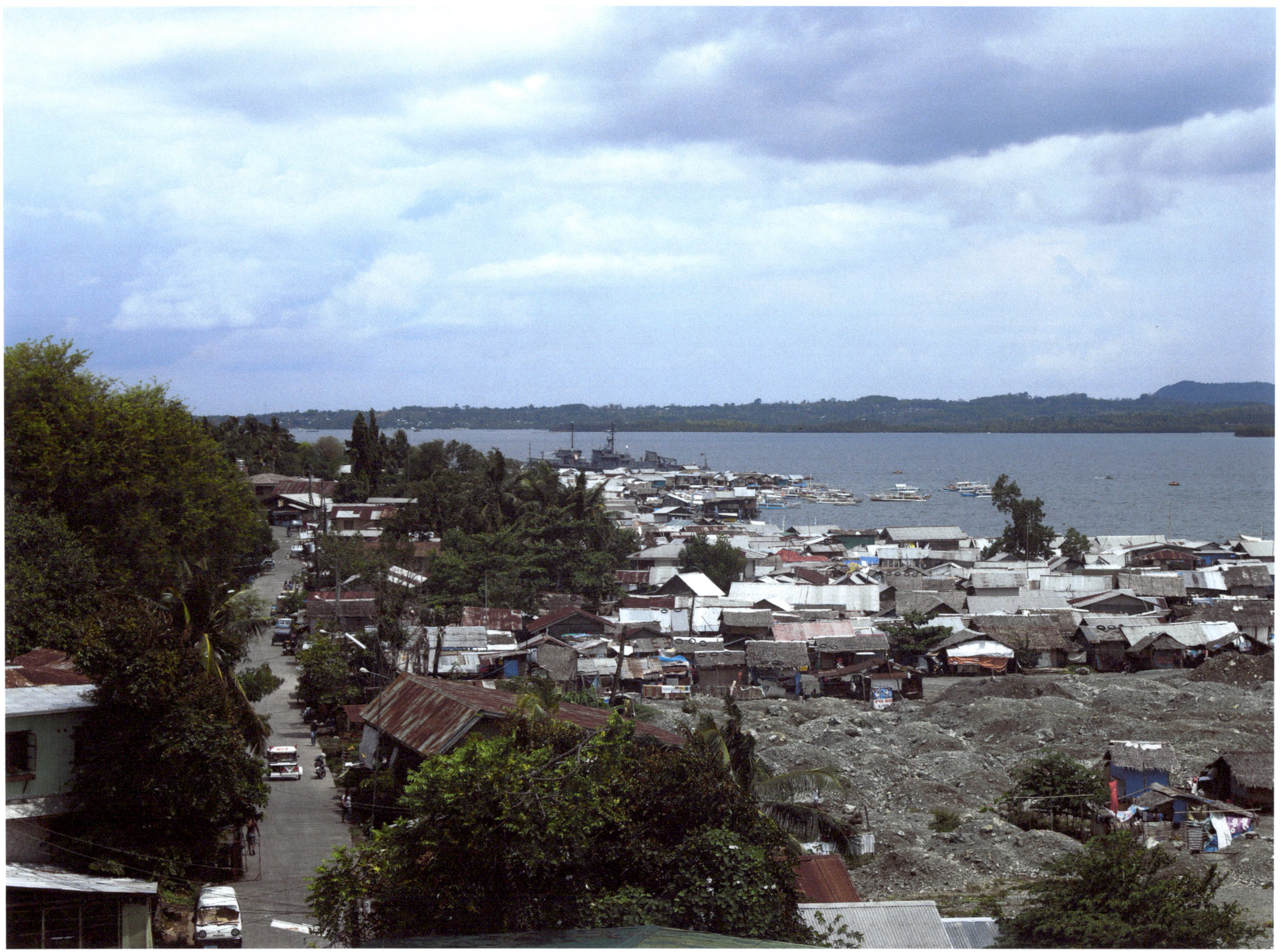

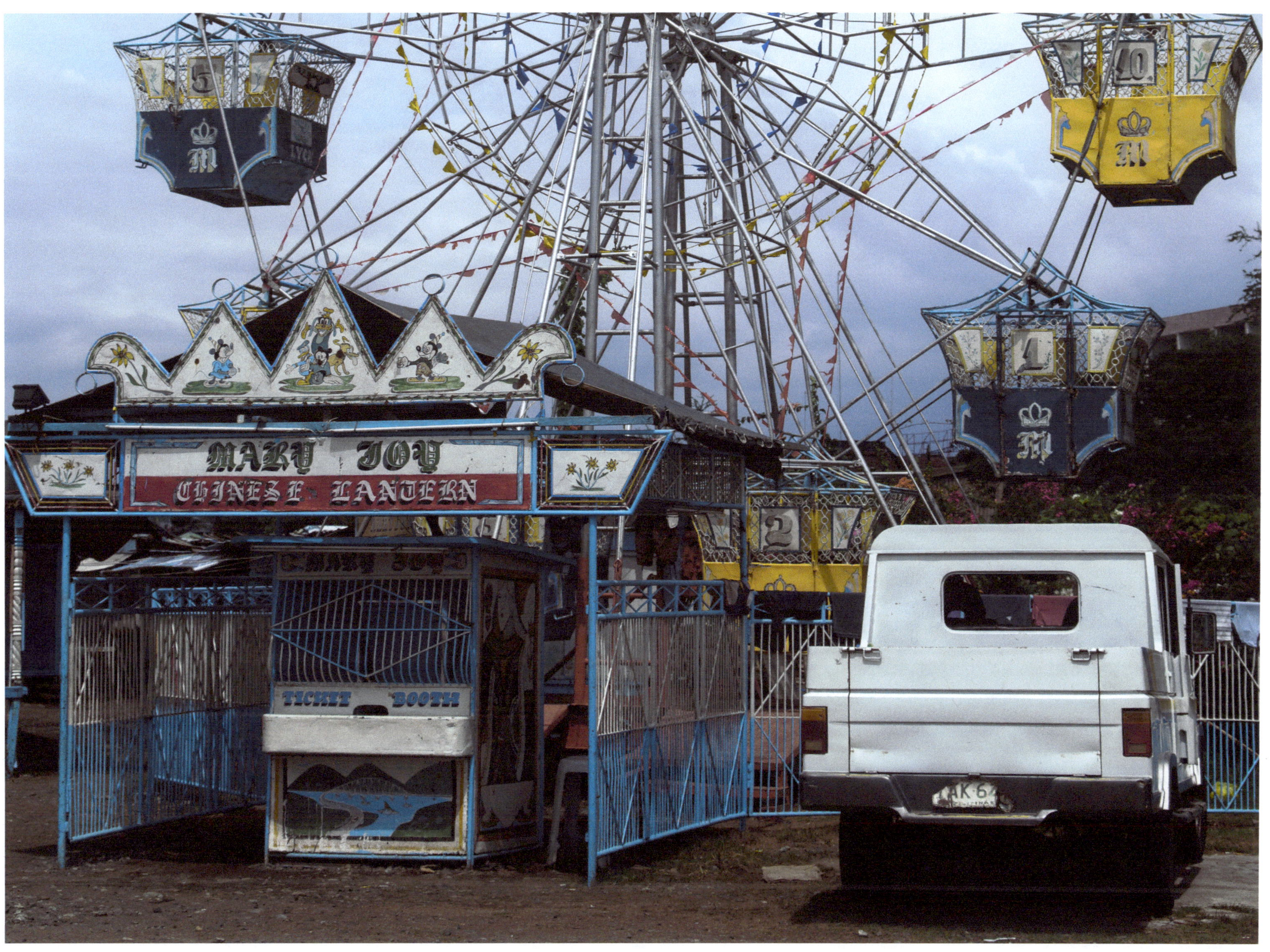
MARY JOY
CHINESE LANTERN
TICKET BOOTH

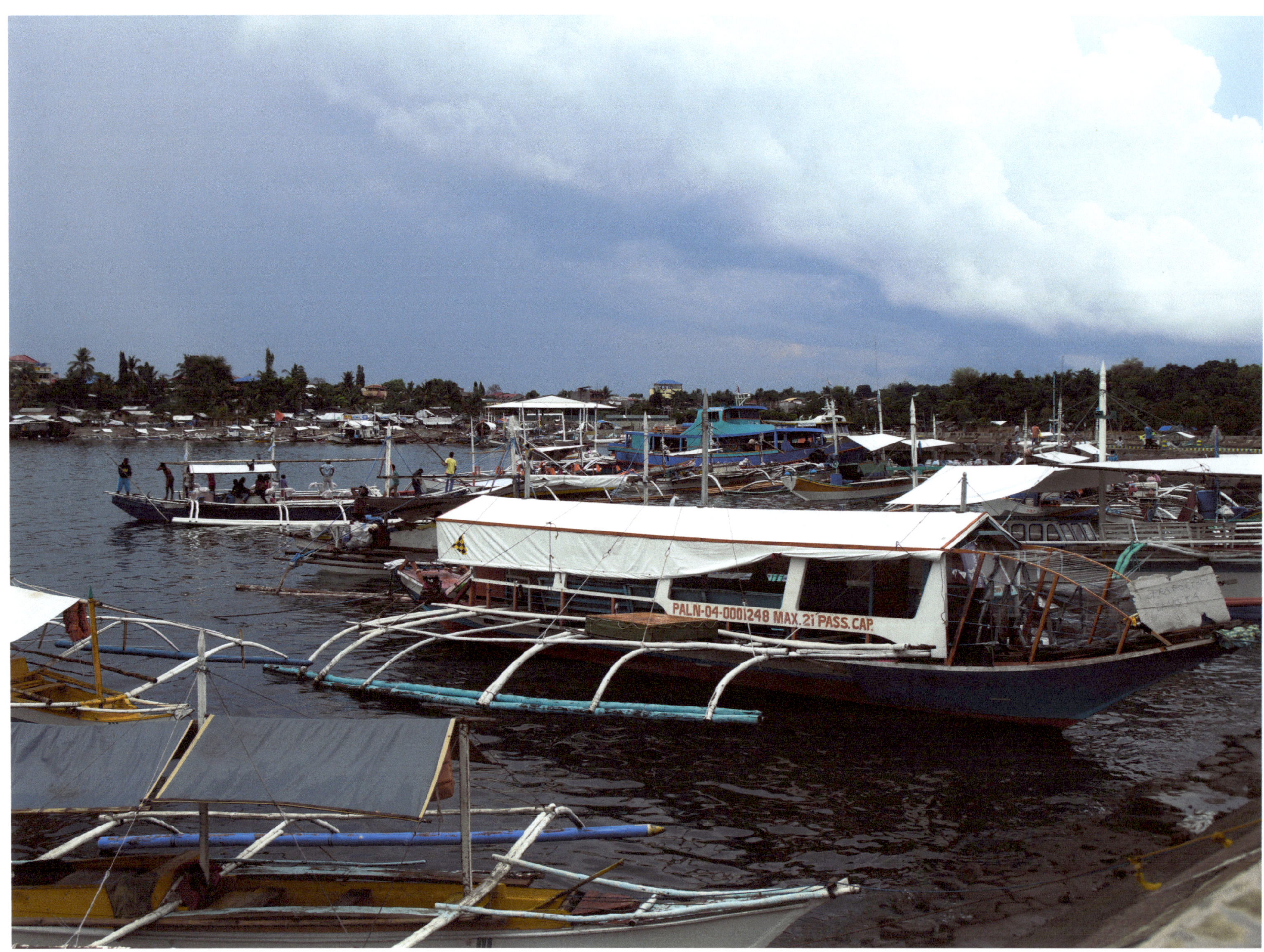
PALN-04-0001248 MAX. 21 PASS. CAP.

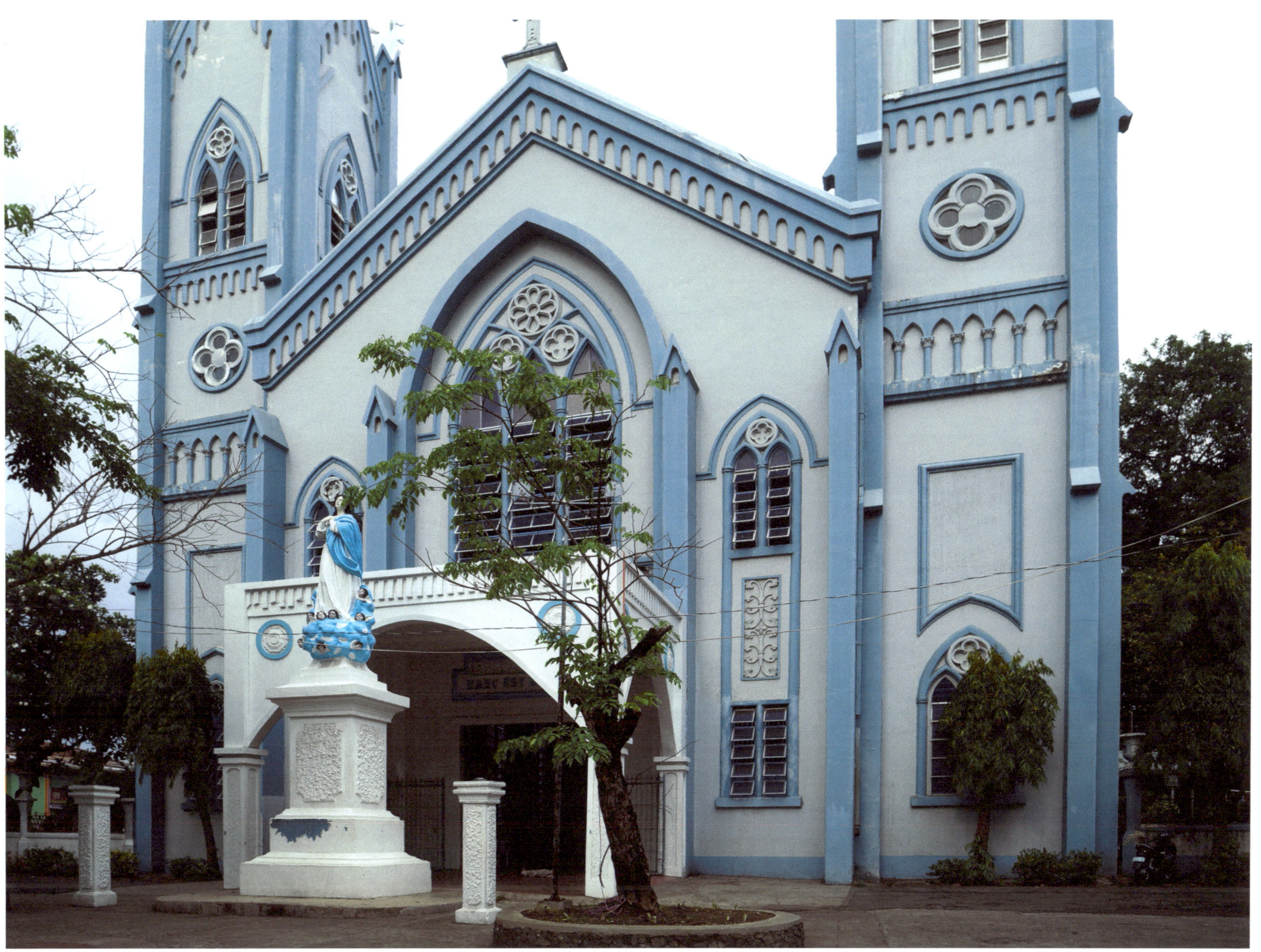

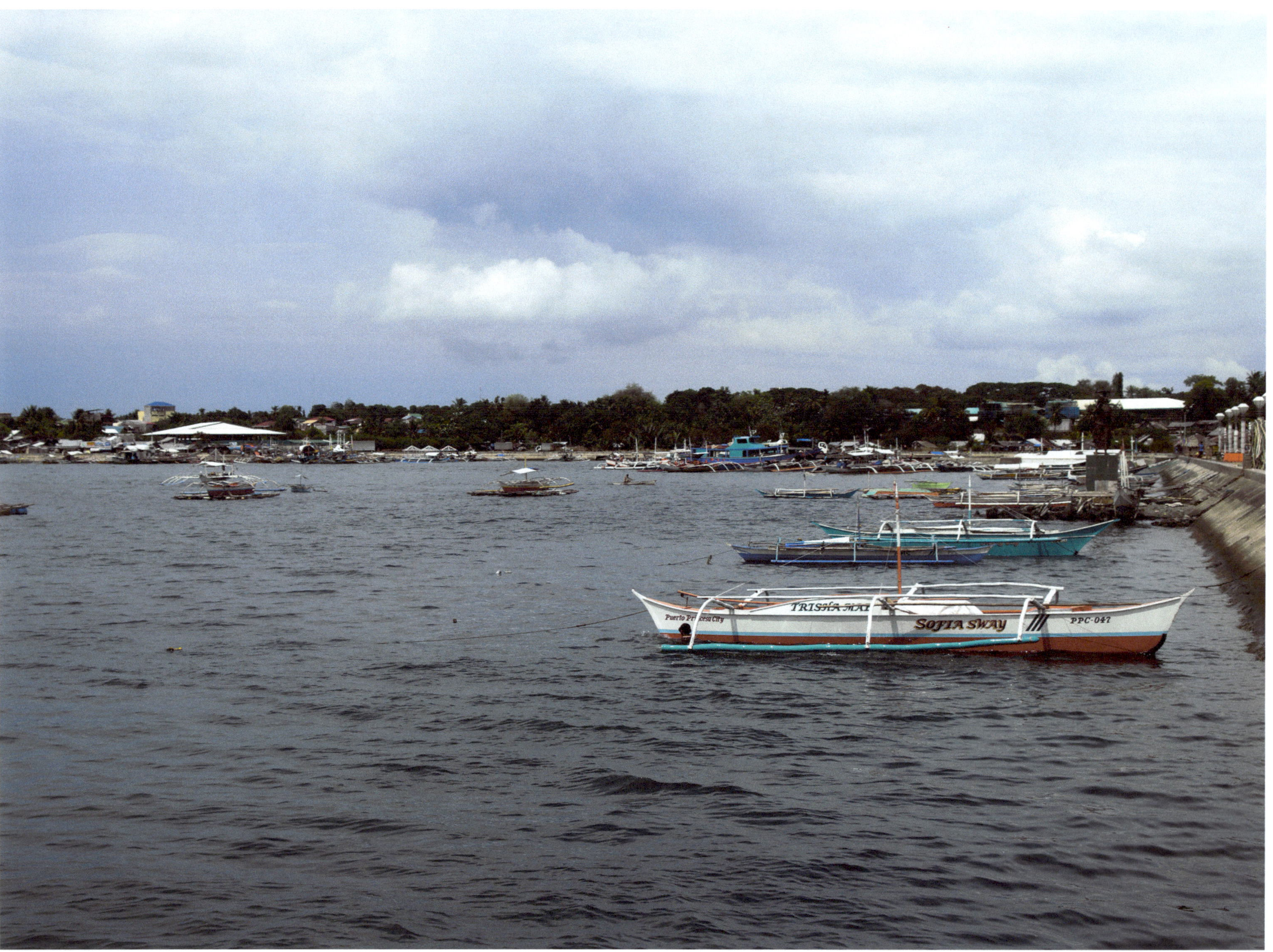
SOFIA SWAY
PPC-047

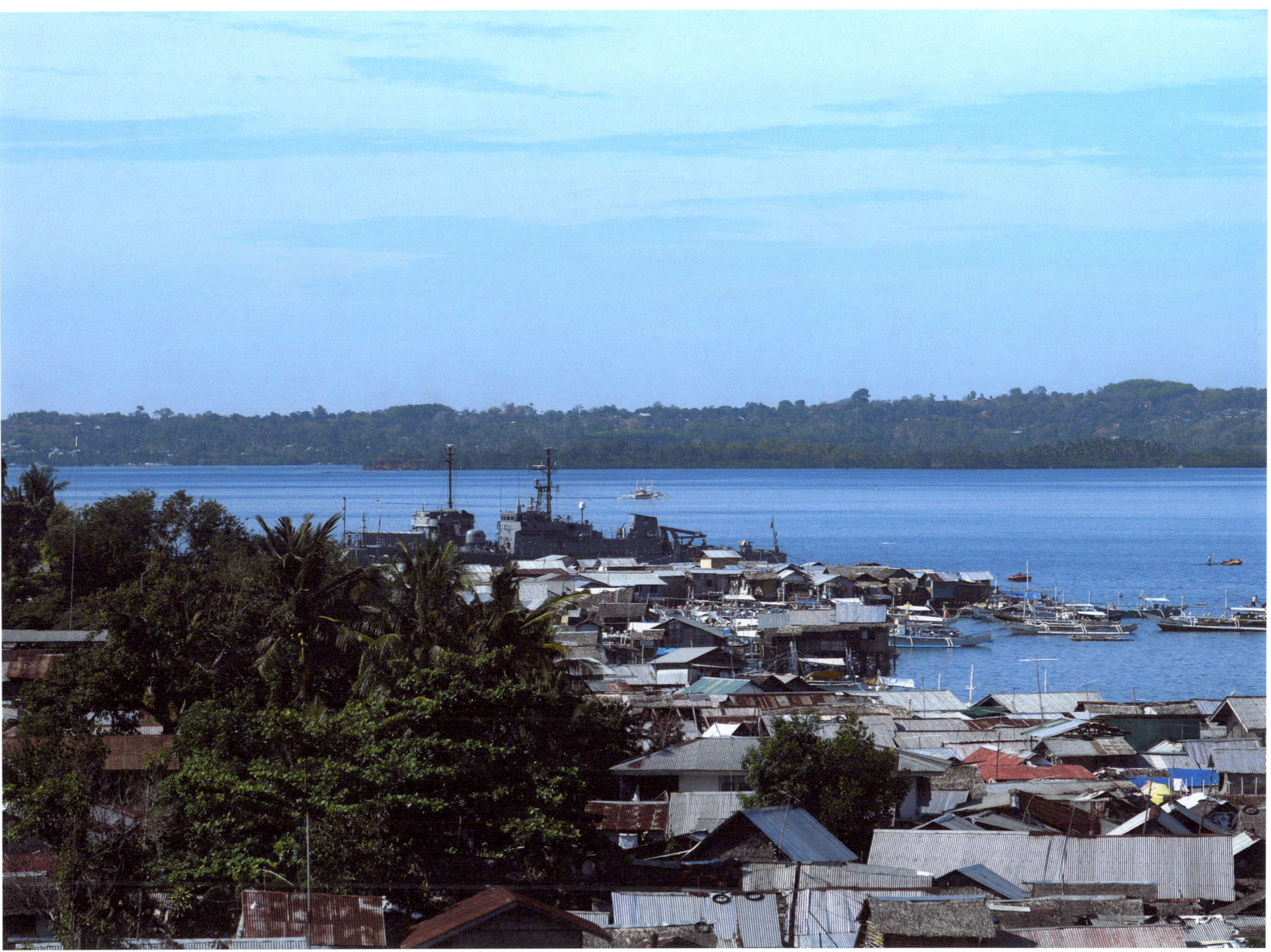

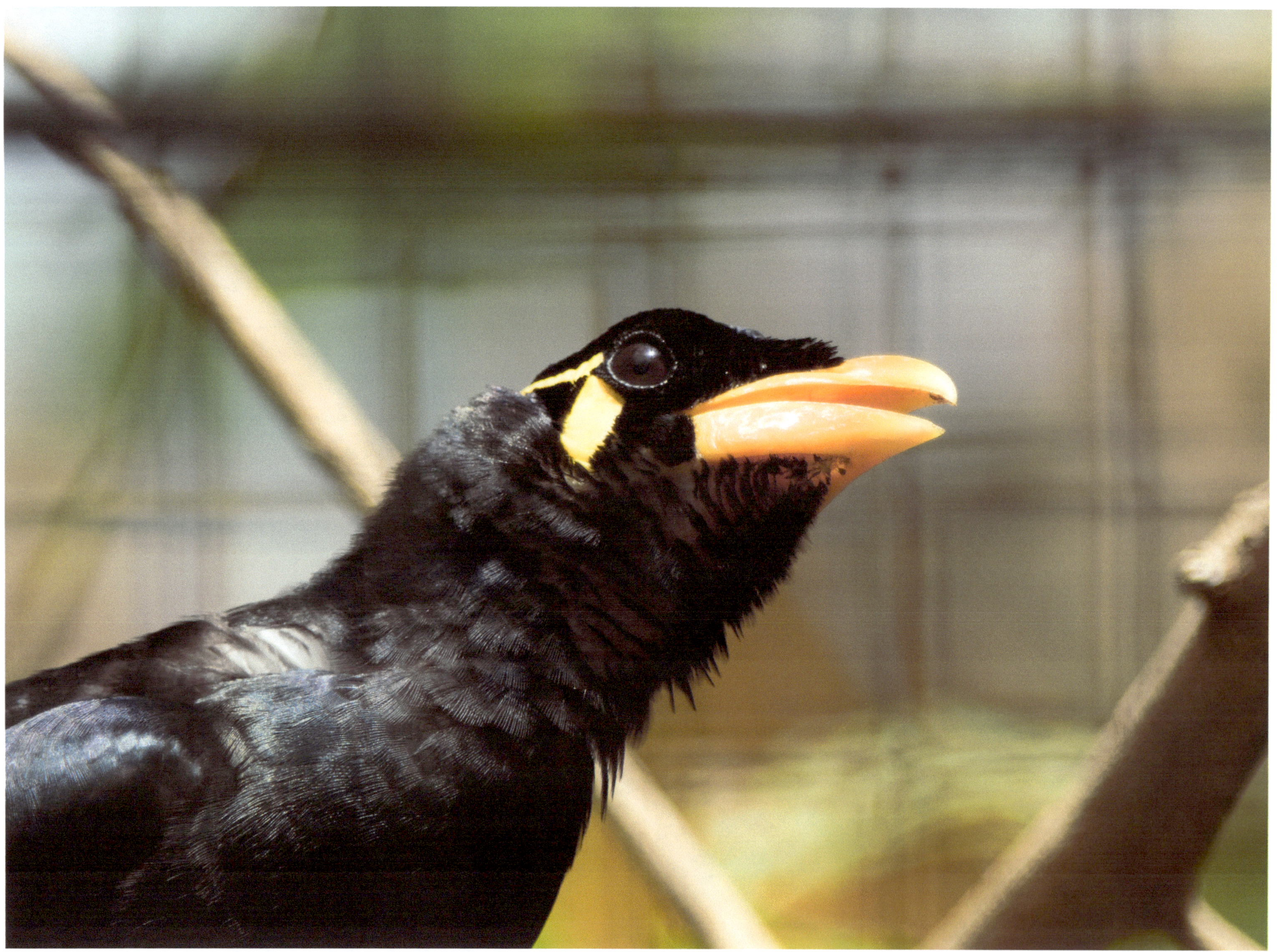

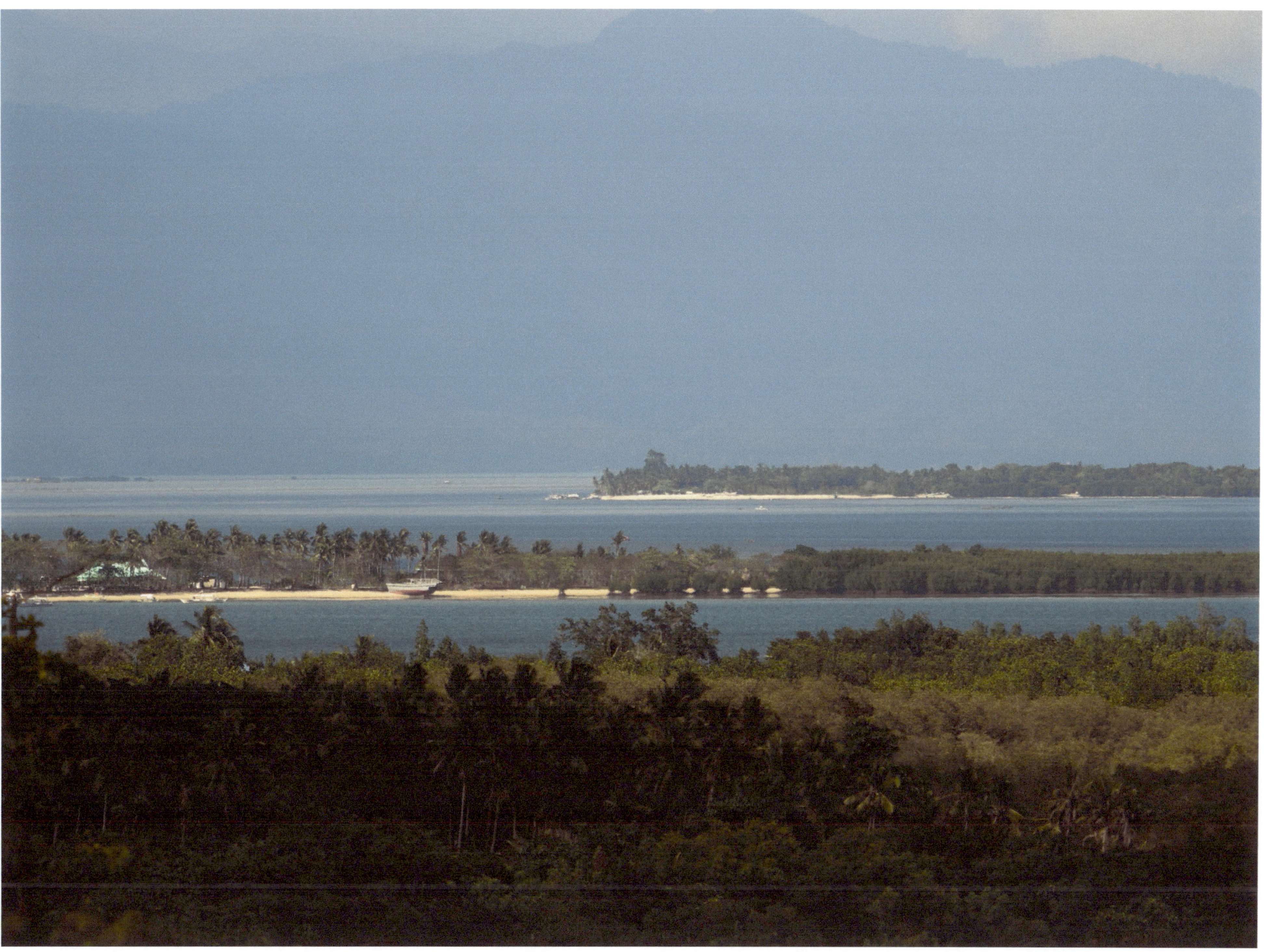

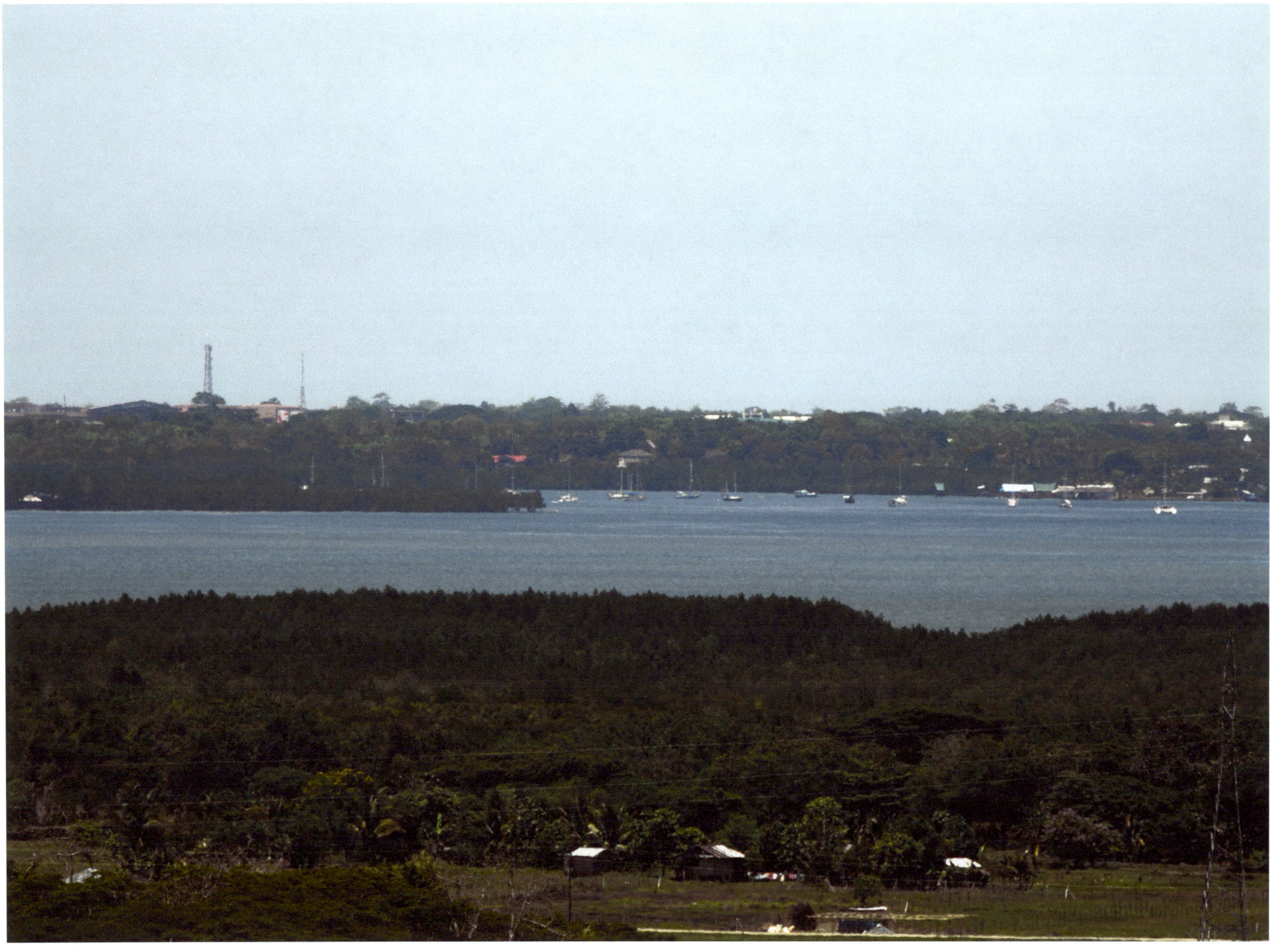

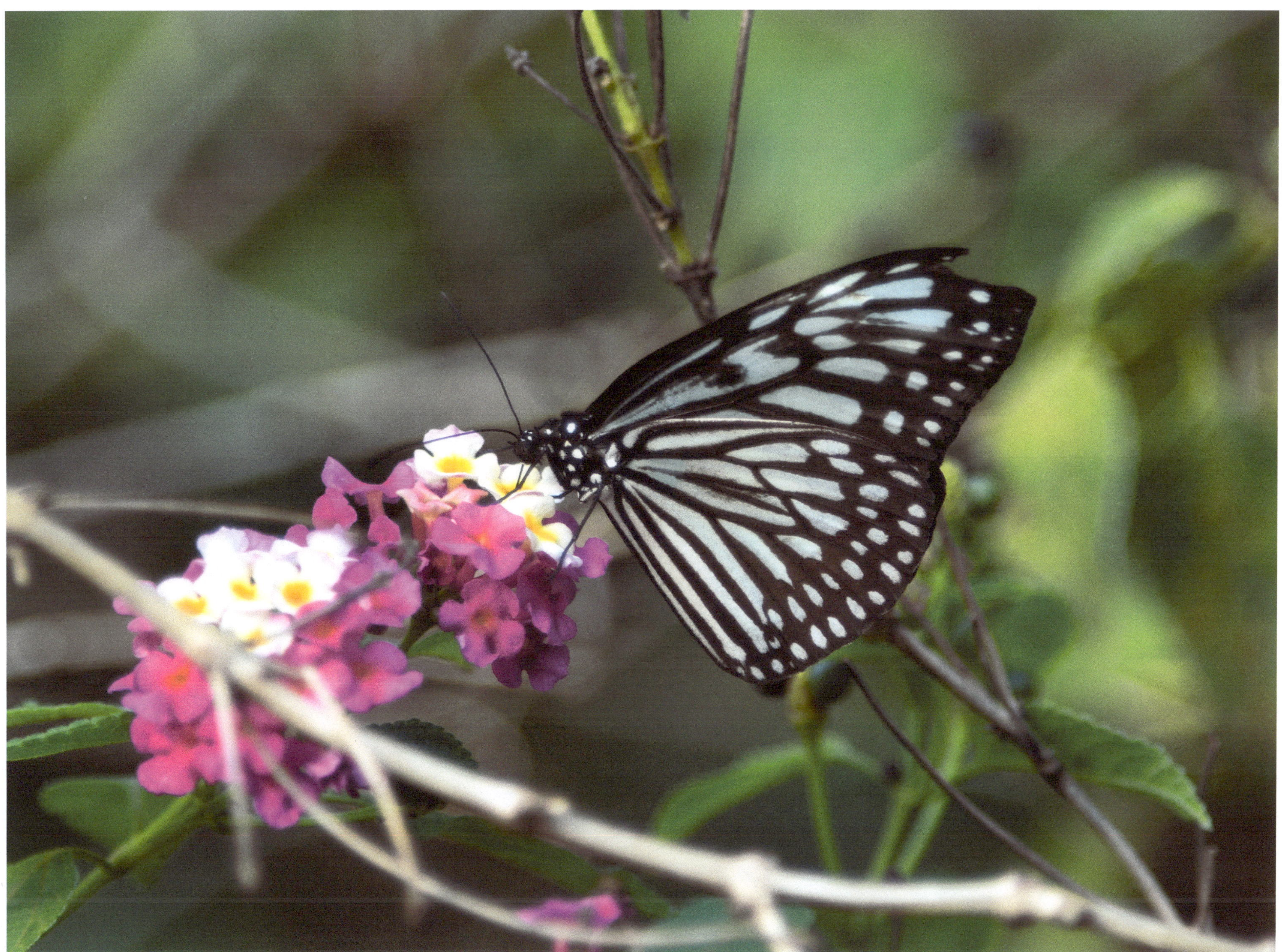

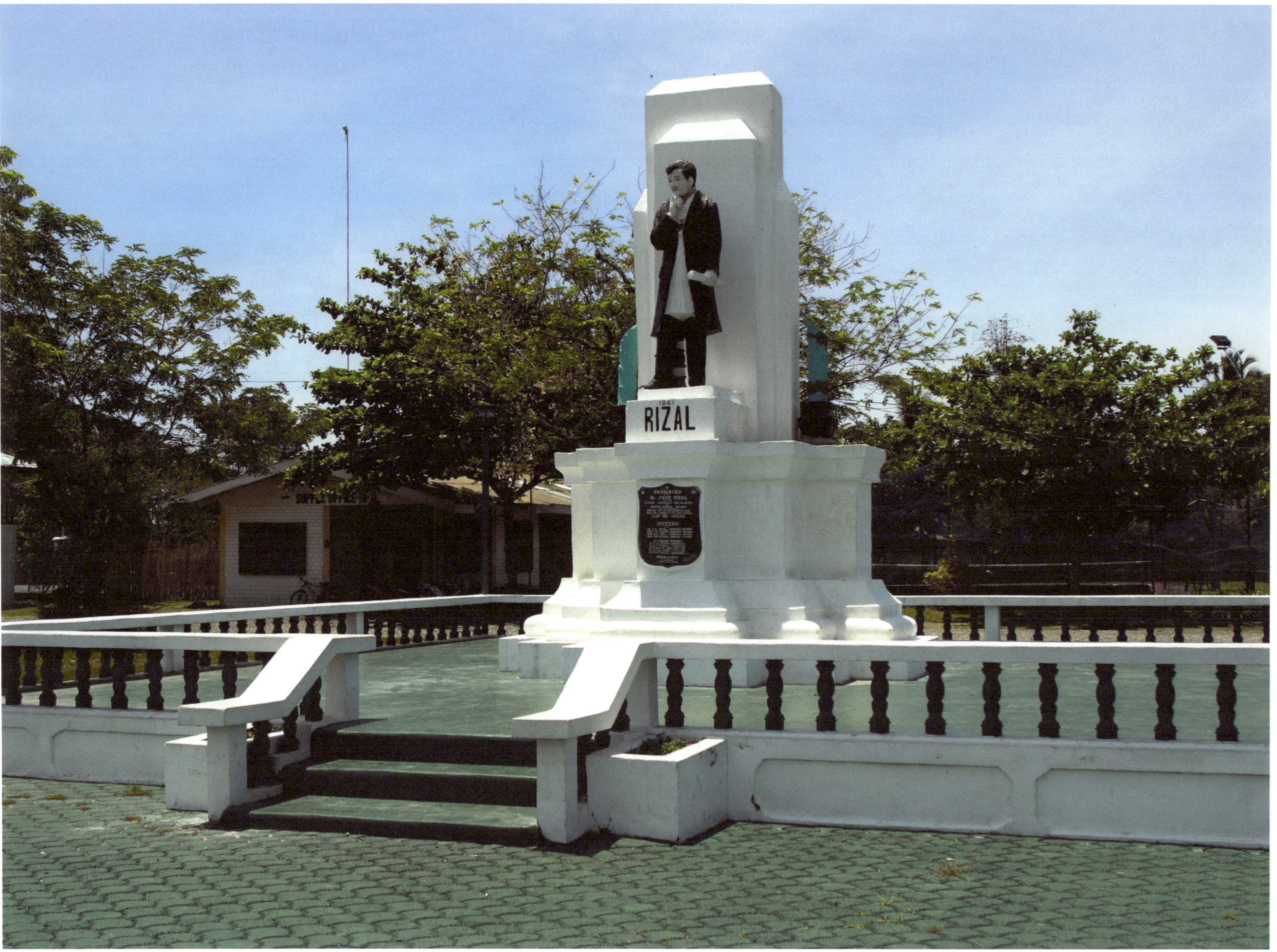
1861
RIZAL
DEDICATED
Dr. JOSE RIZAL
OFFICERS

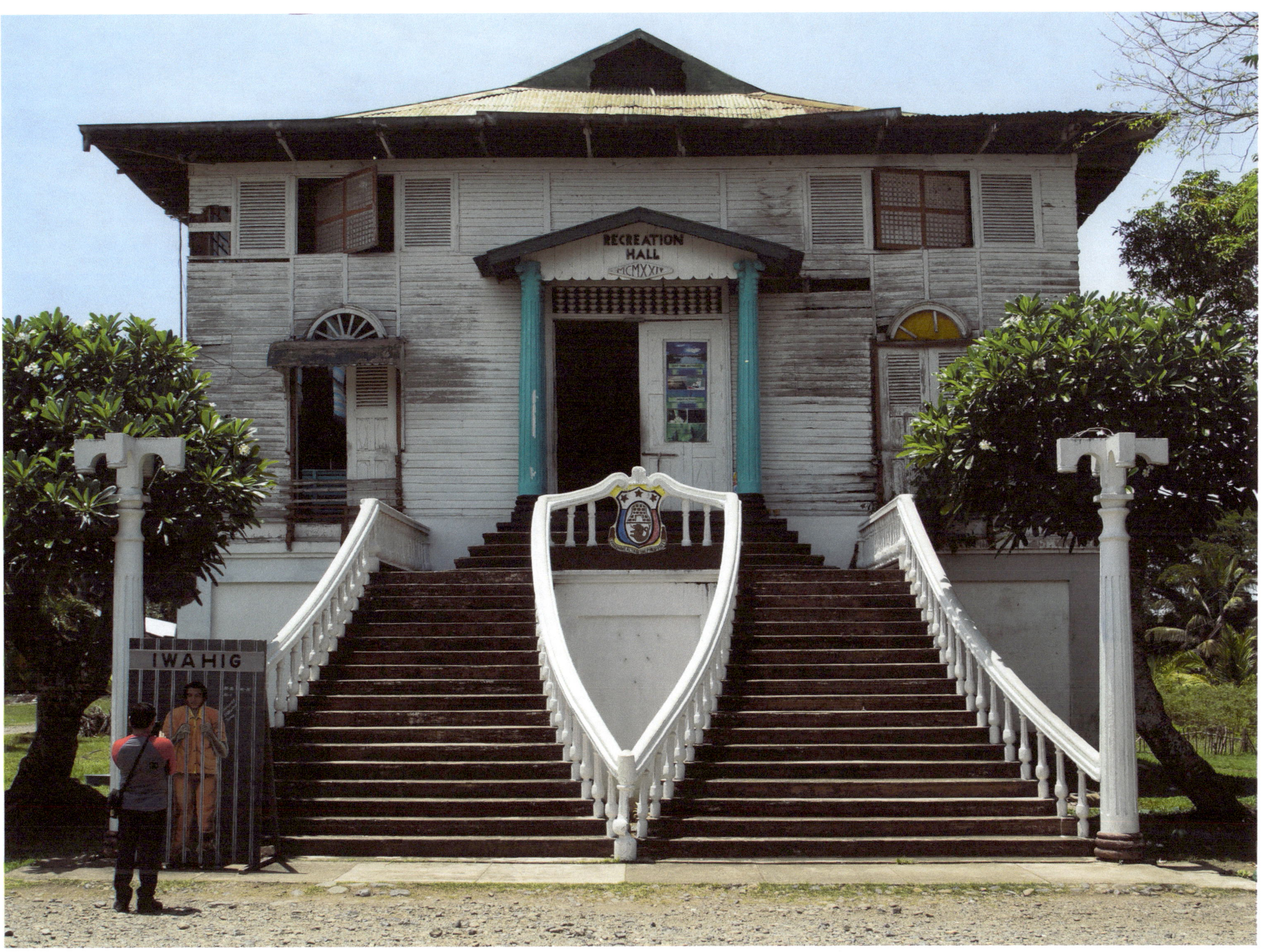
RECREATION
HALL
MCMXXIV
IWAHIG

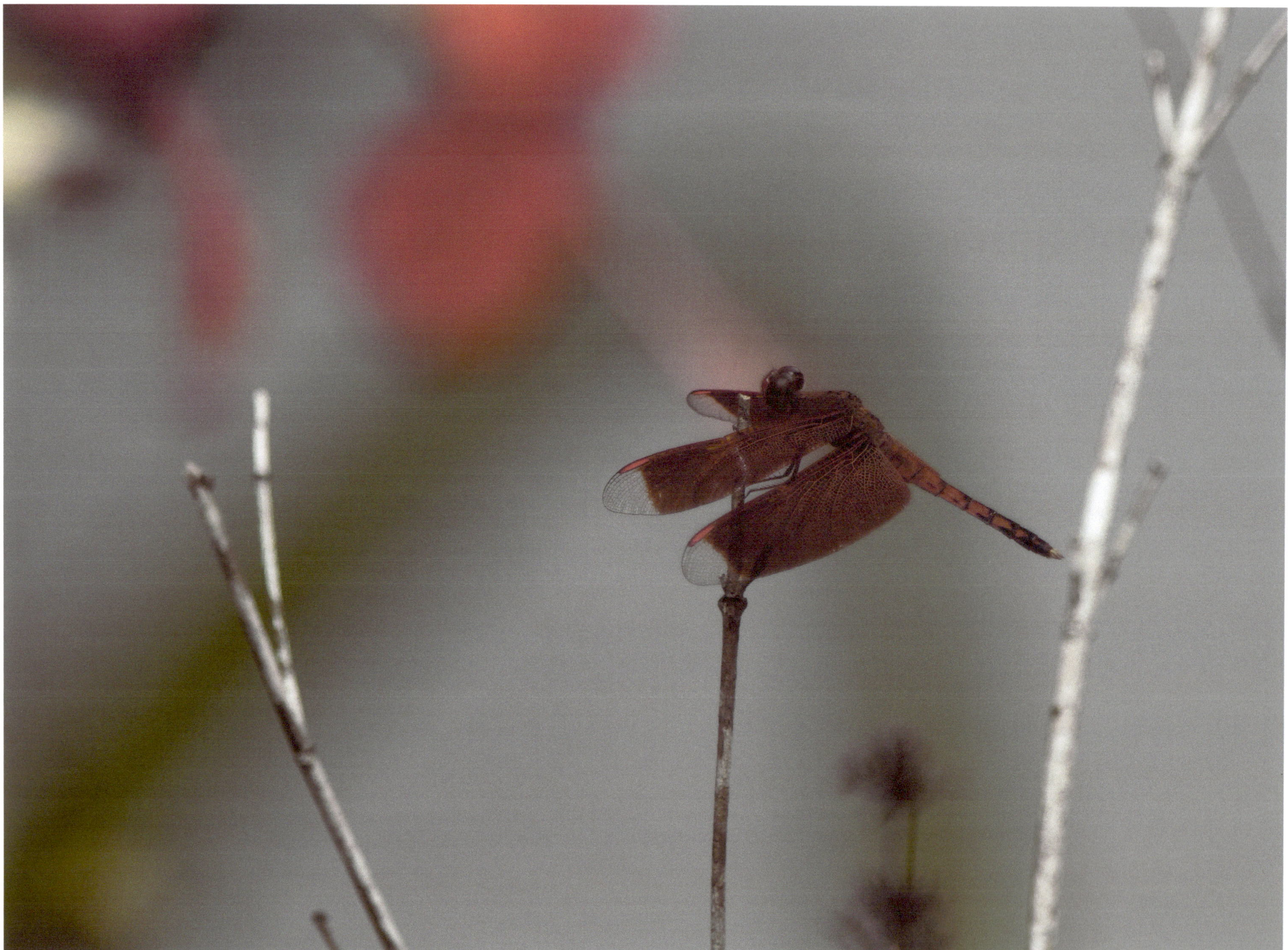

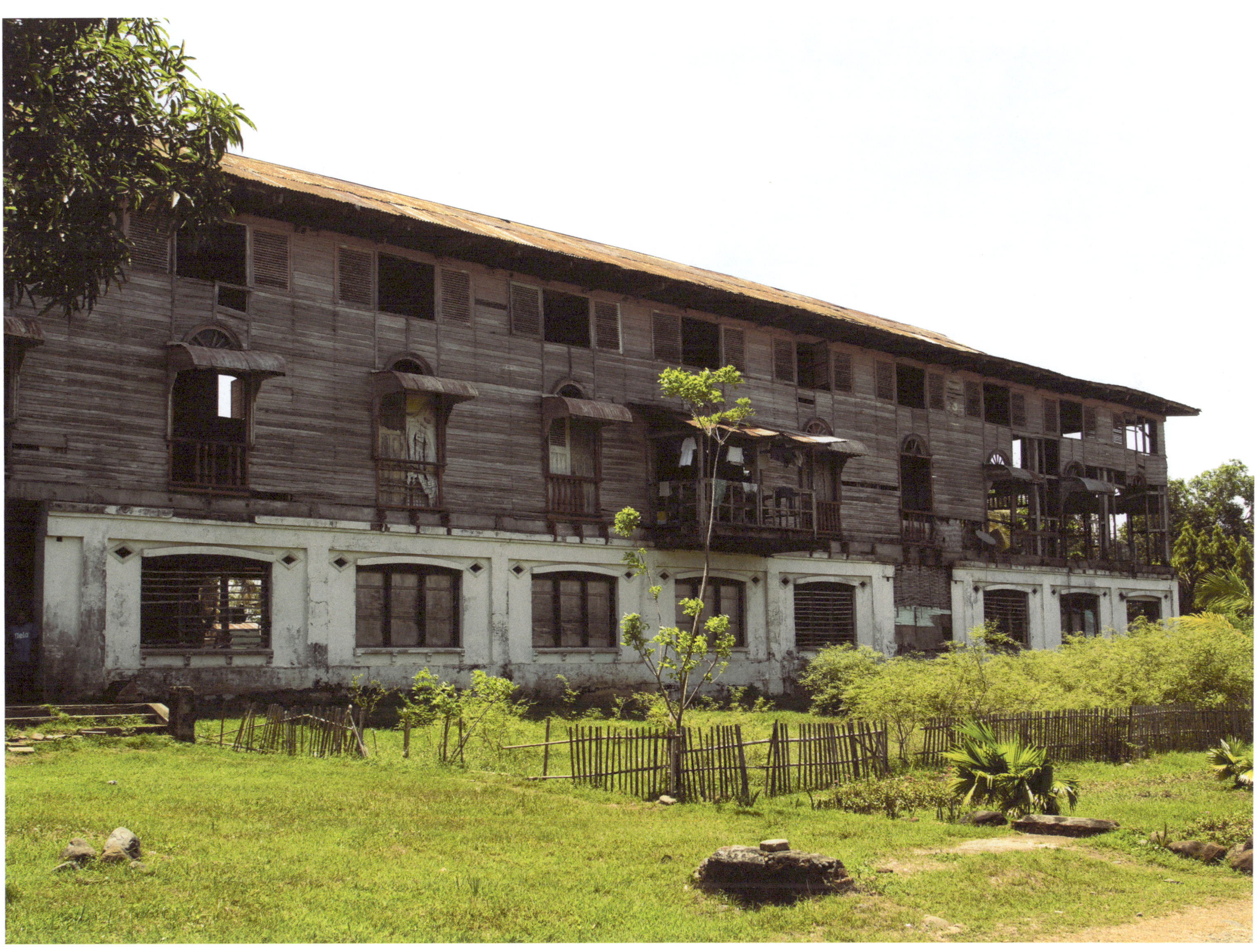

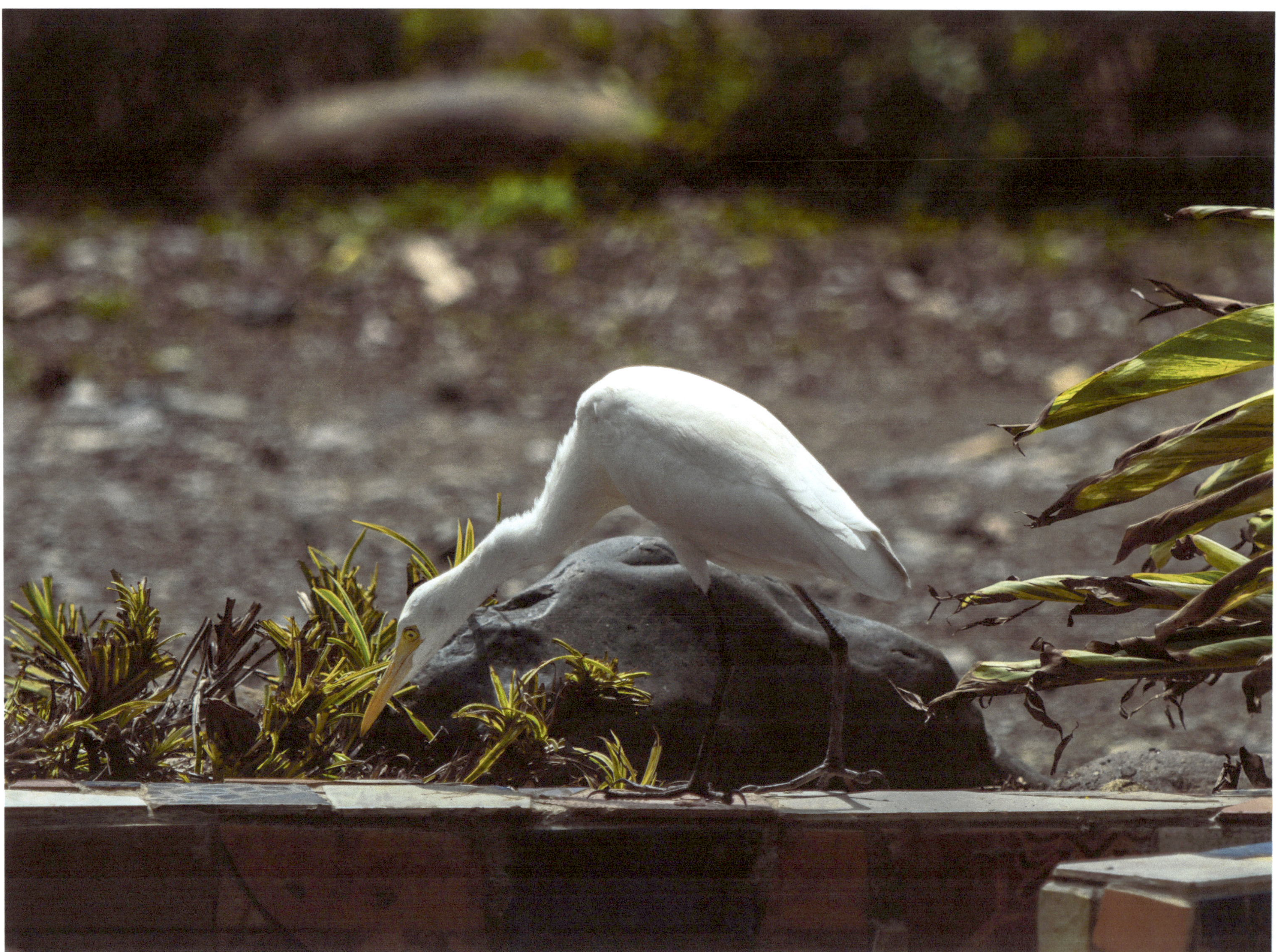

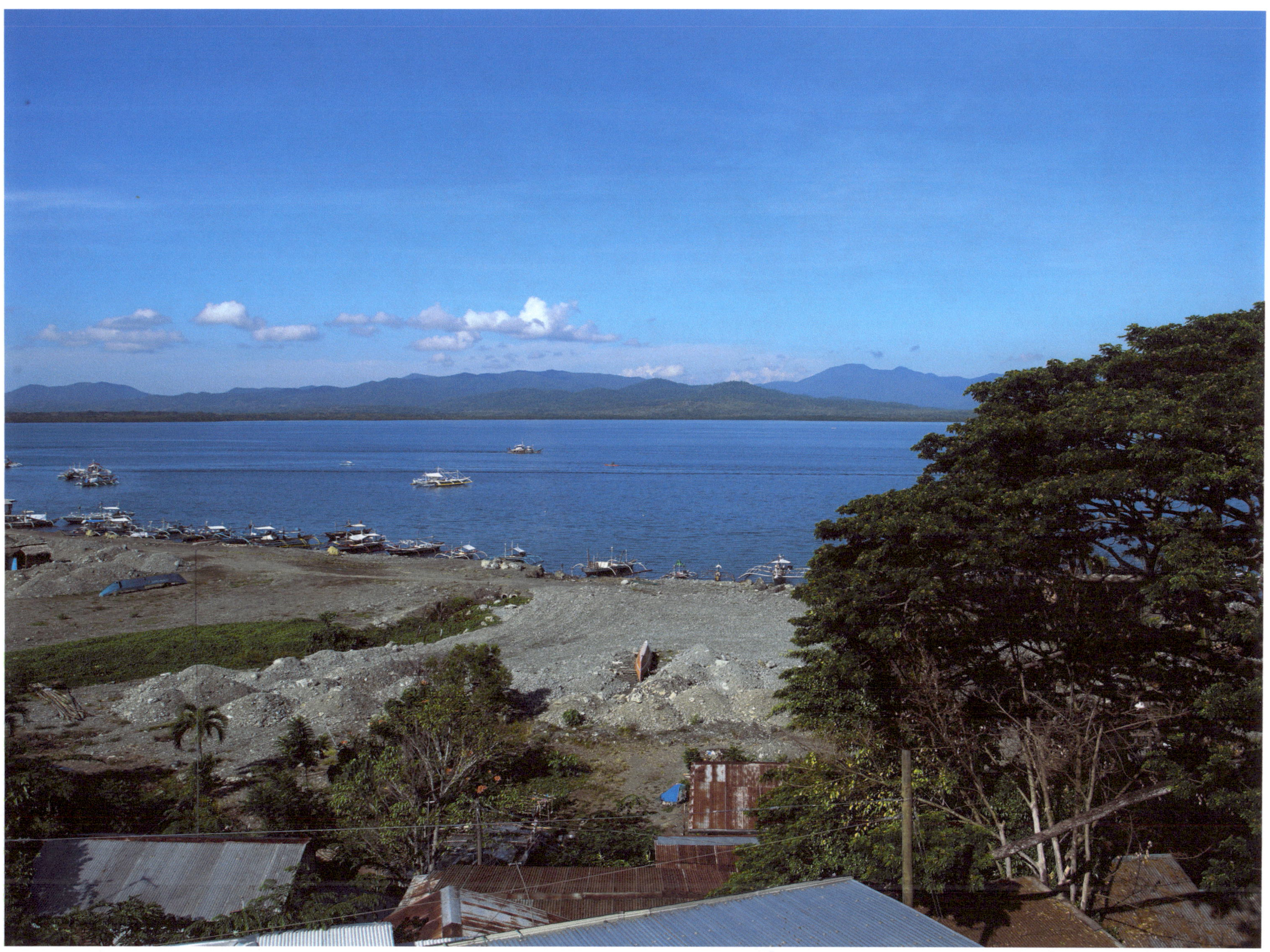

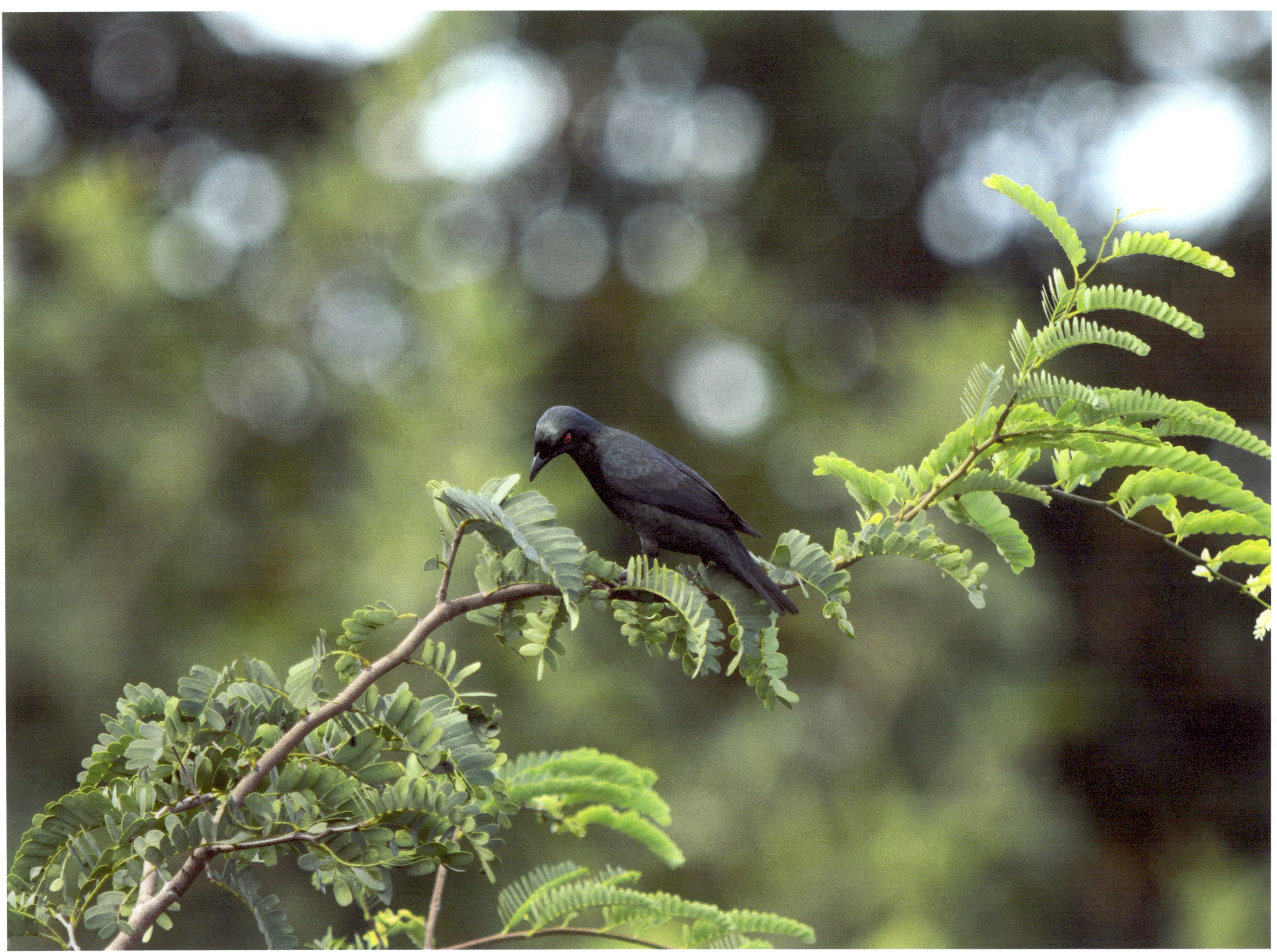

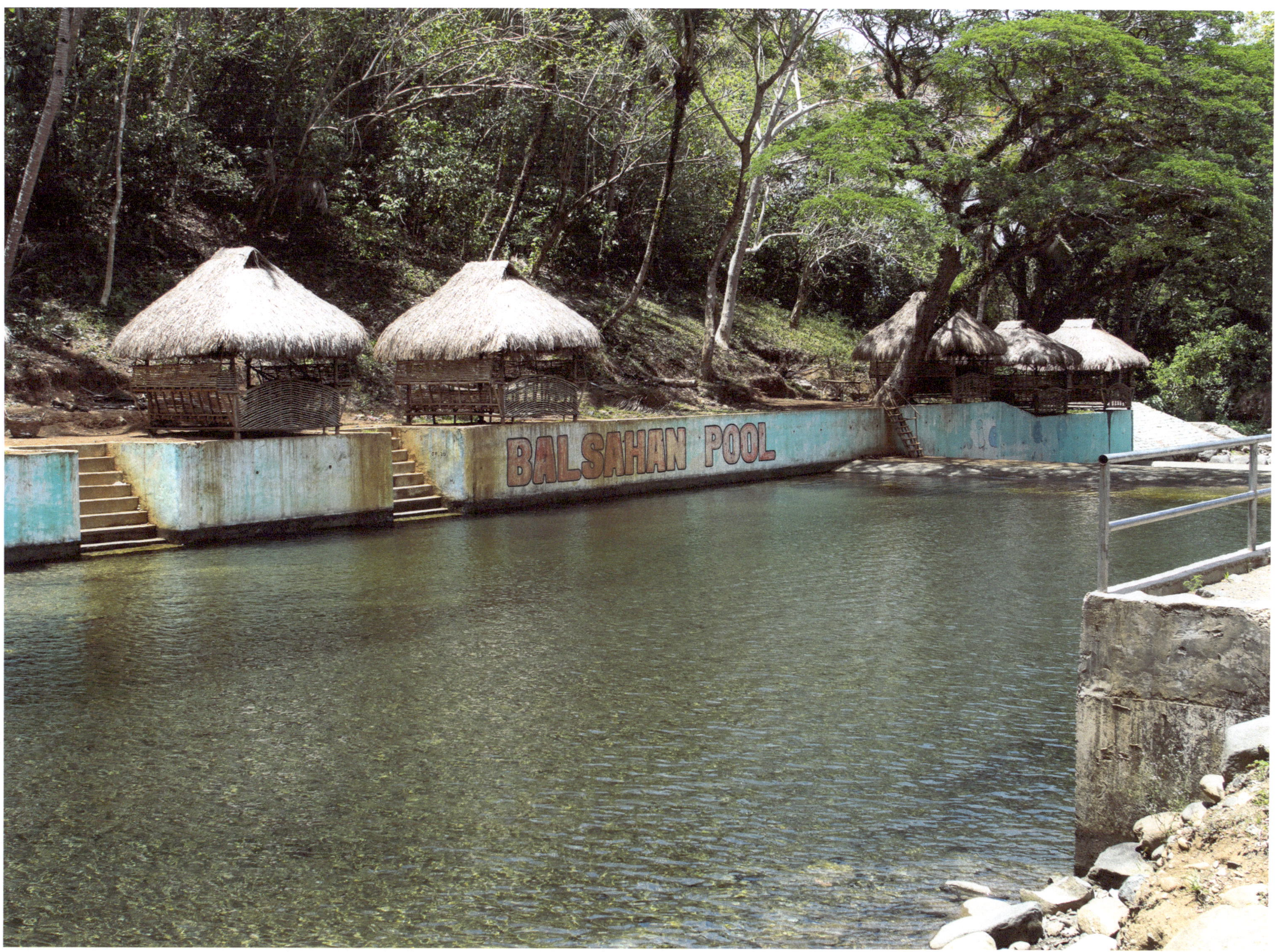
BALSAHAN POOL

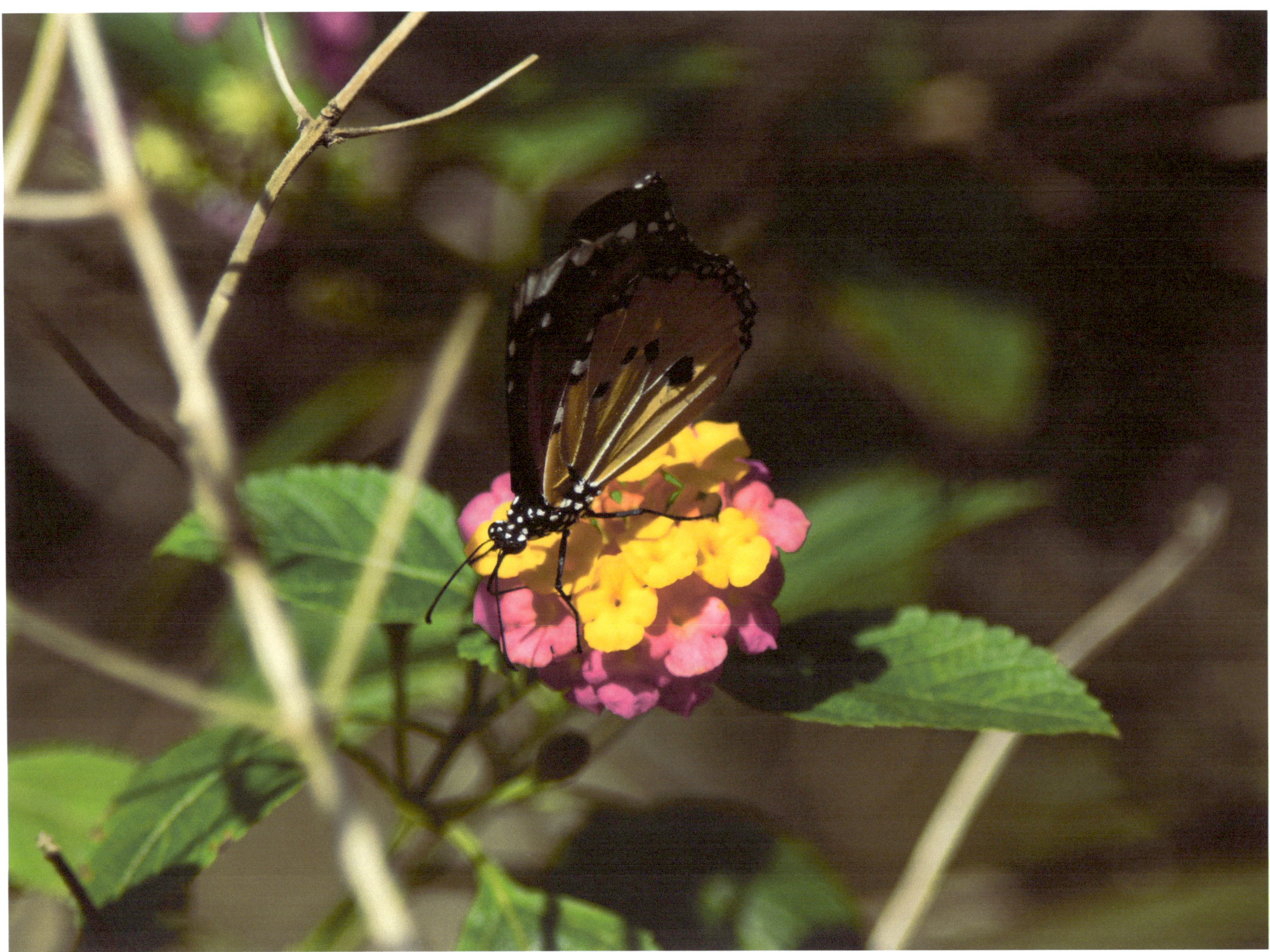

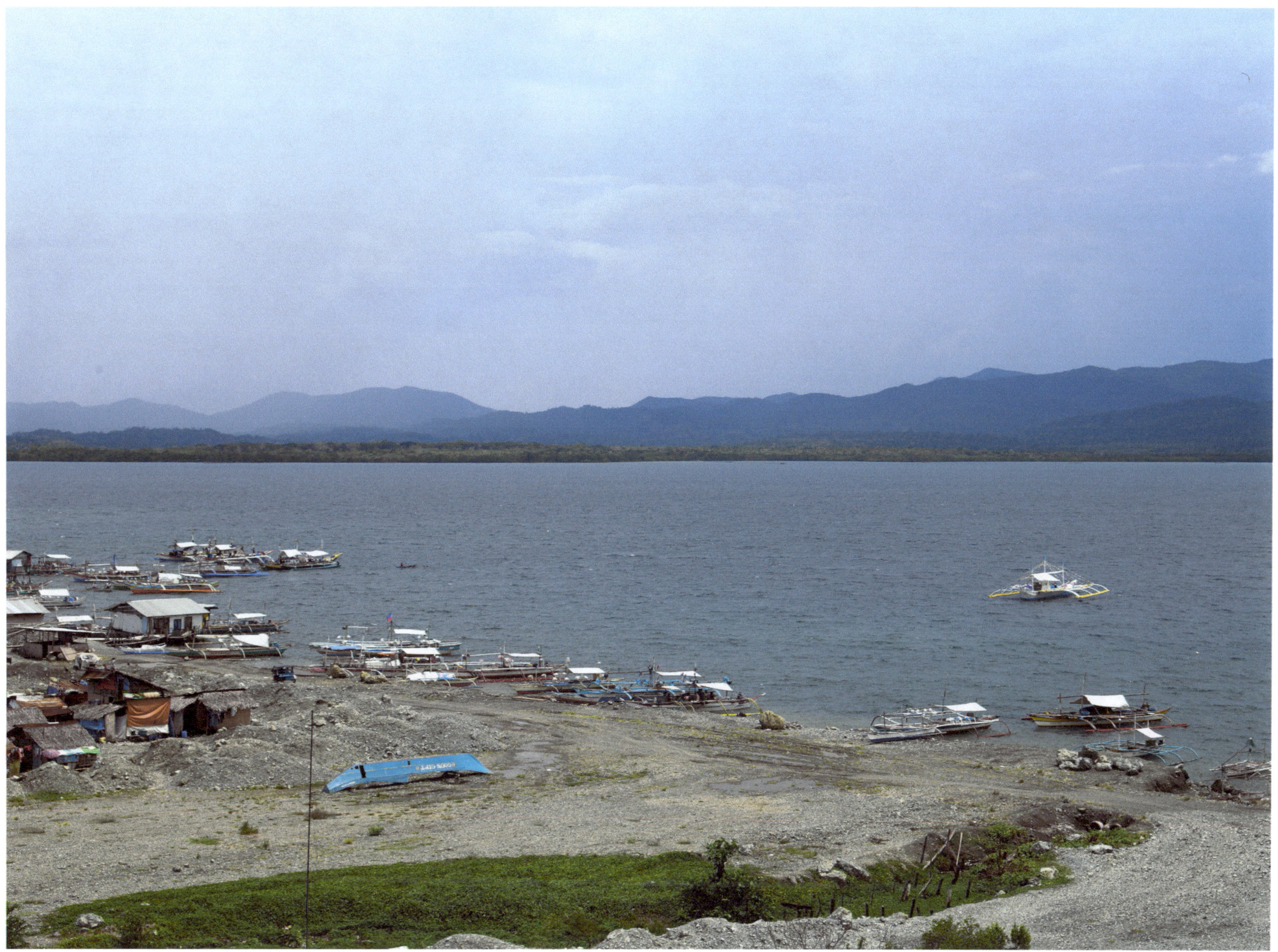

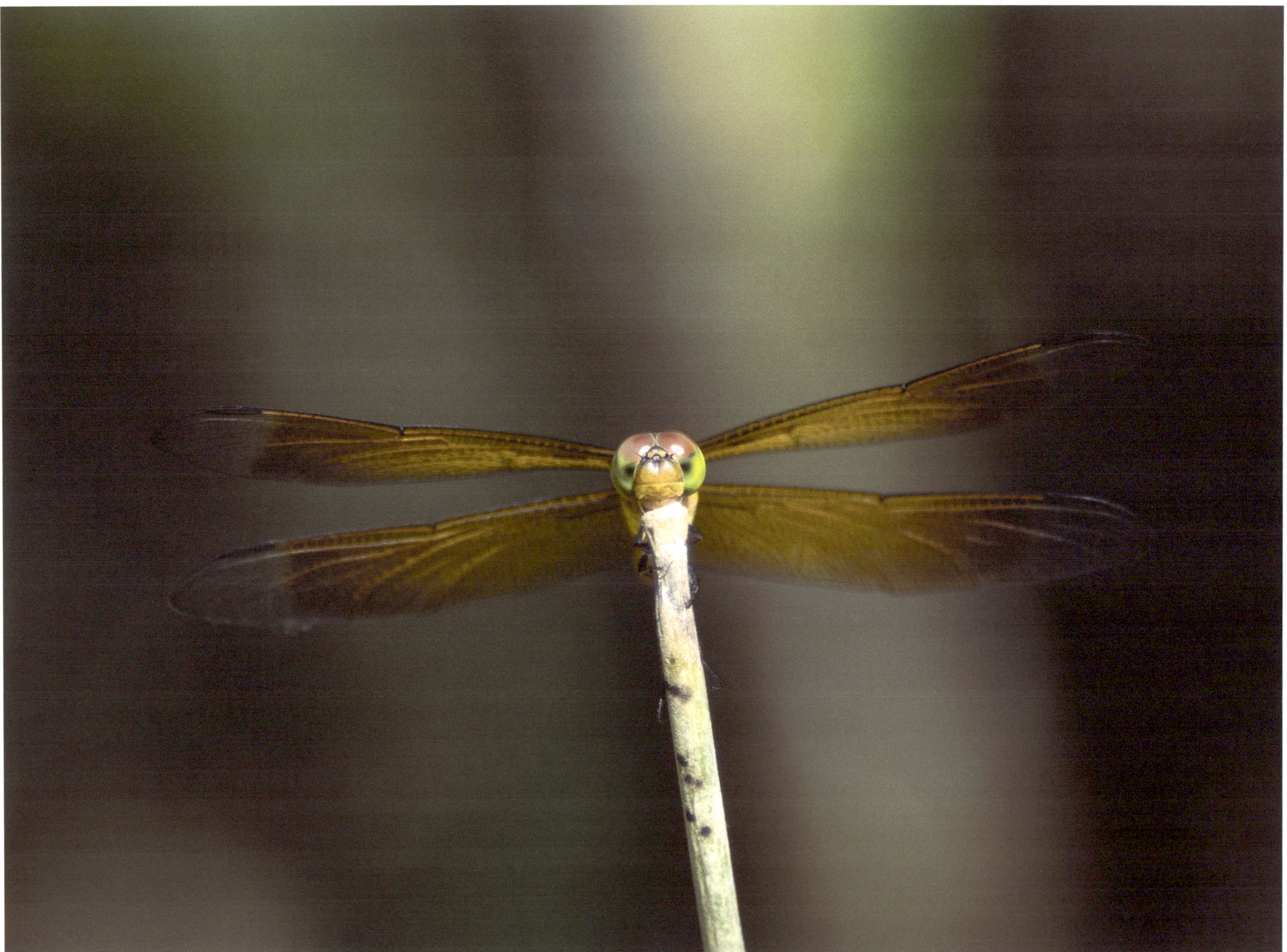

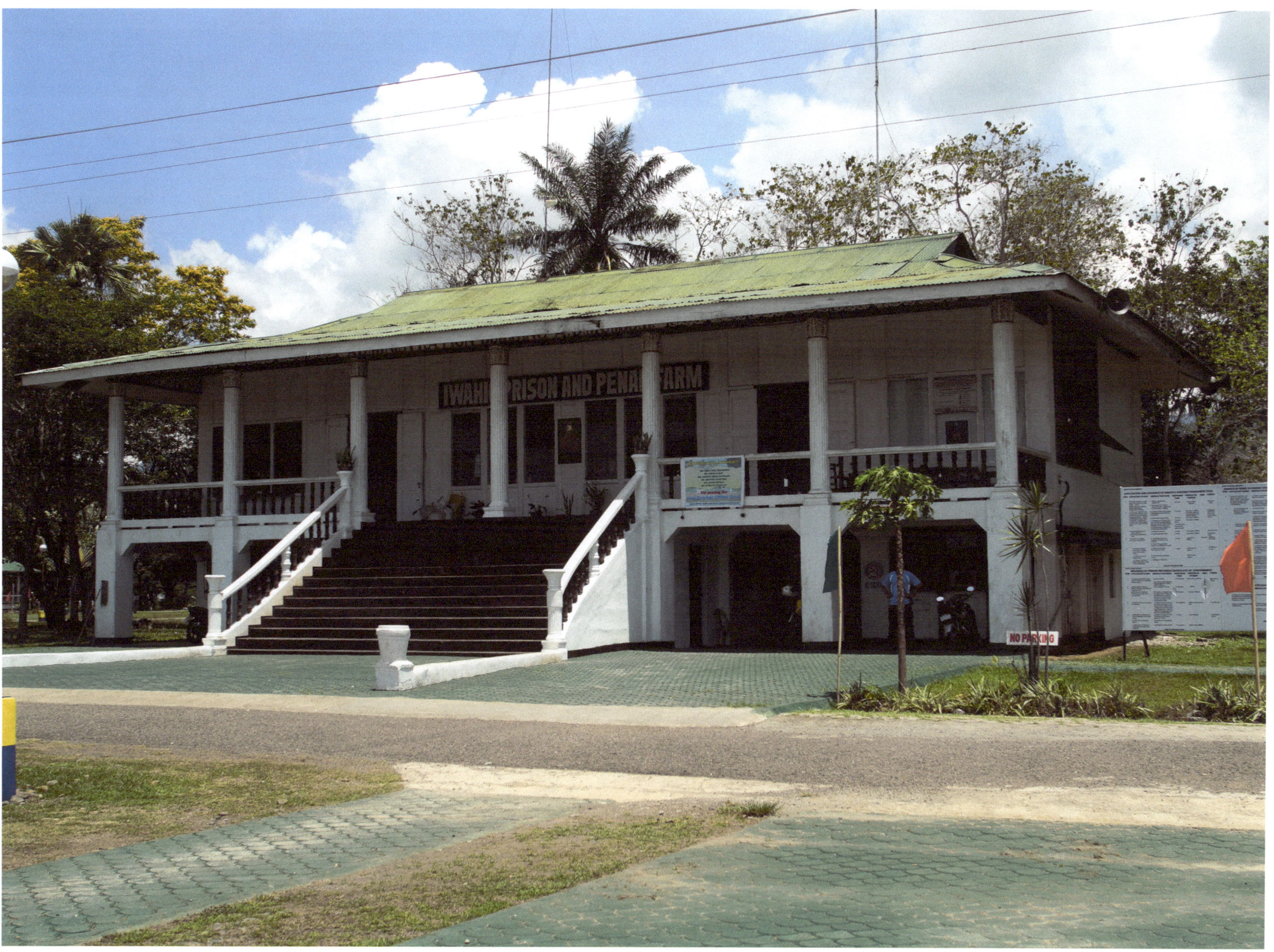
IWAHI
PRISON AND PENA
FARM
NO PARKING

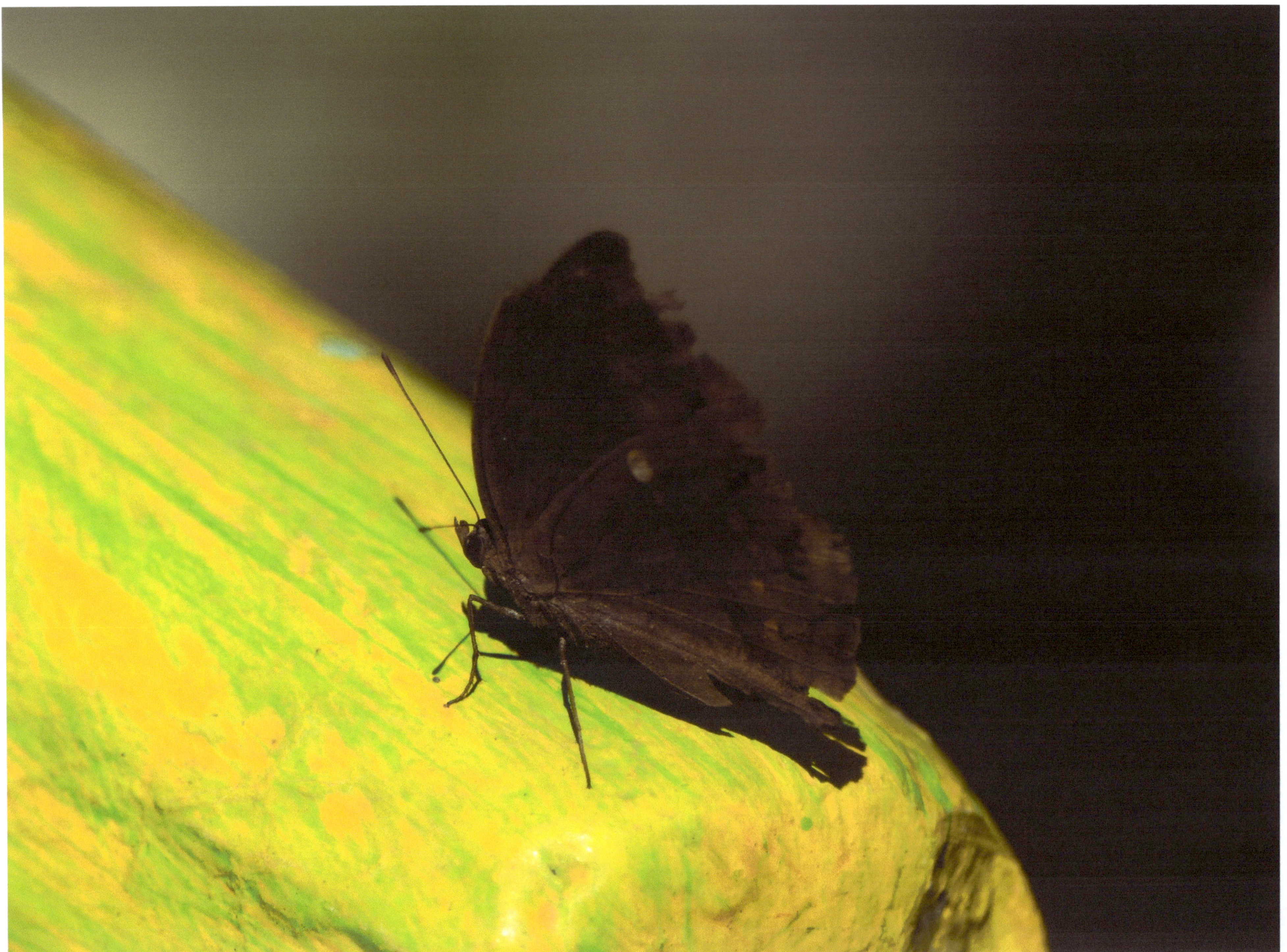

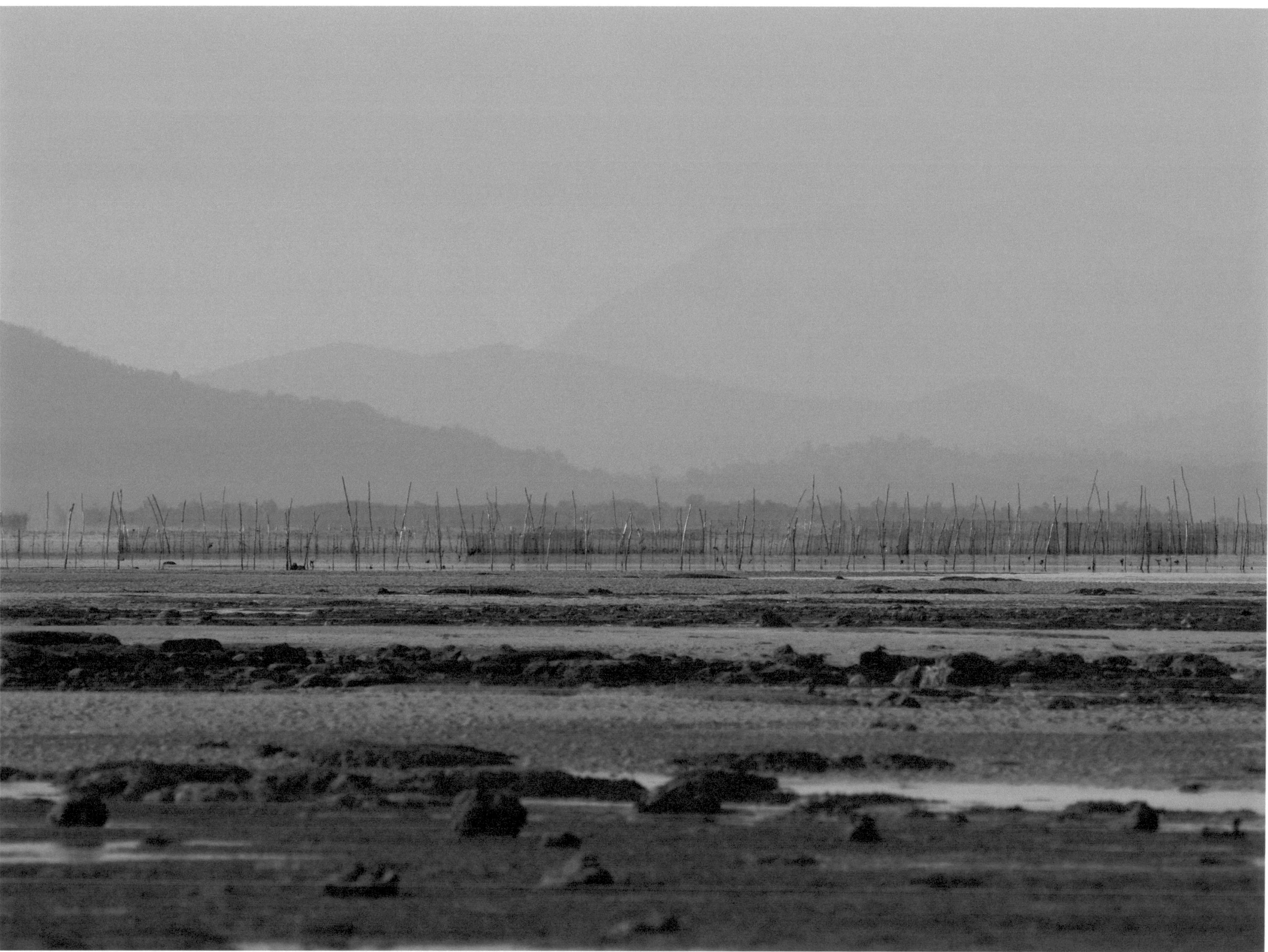

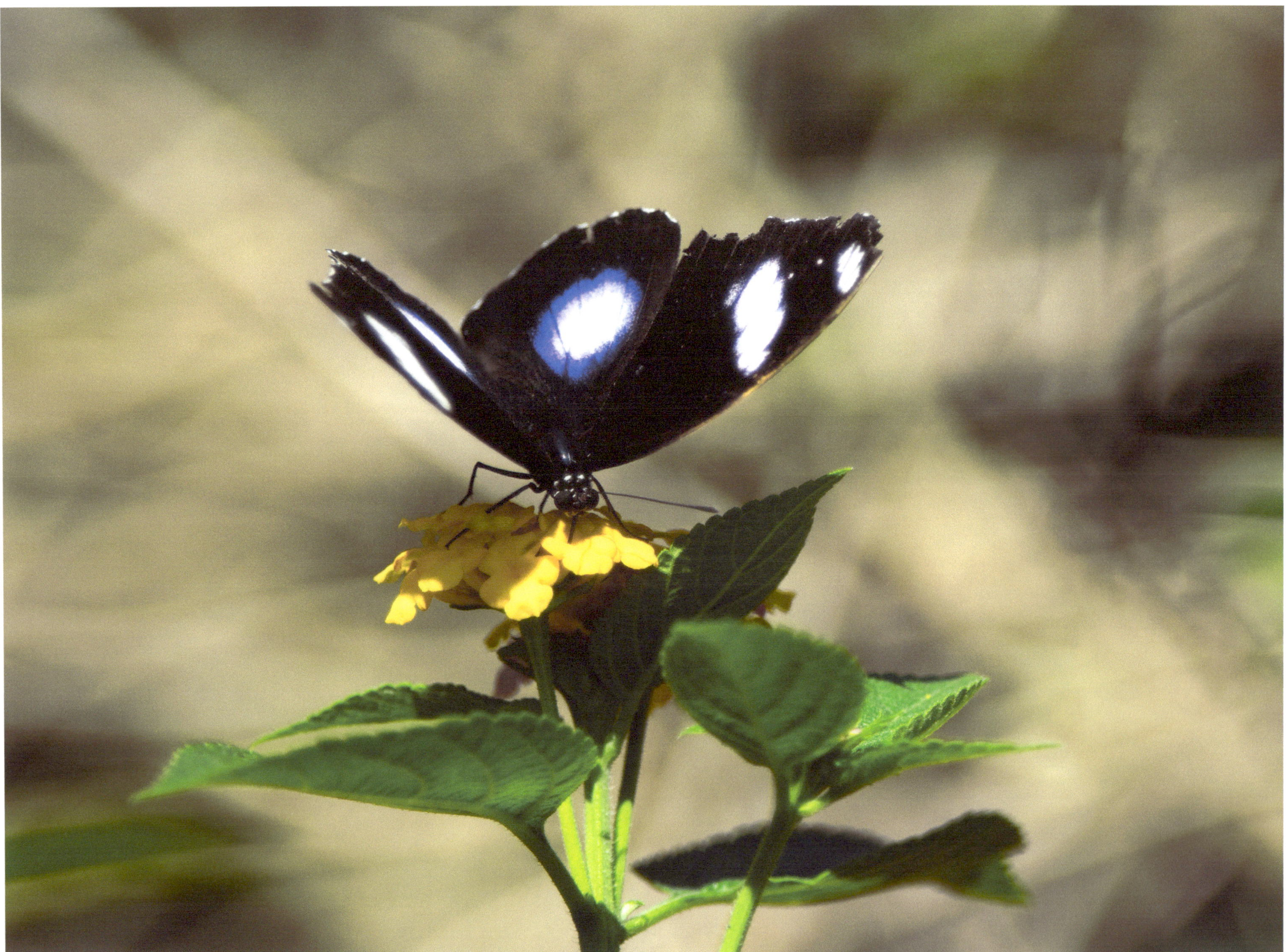

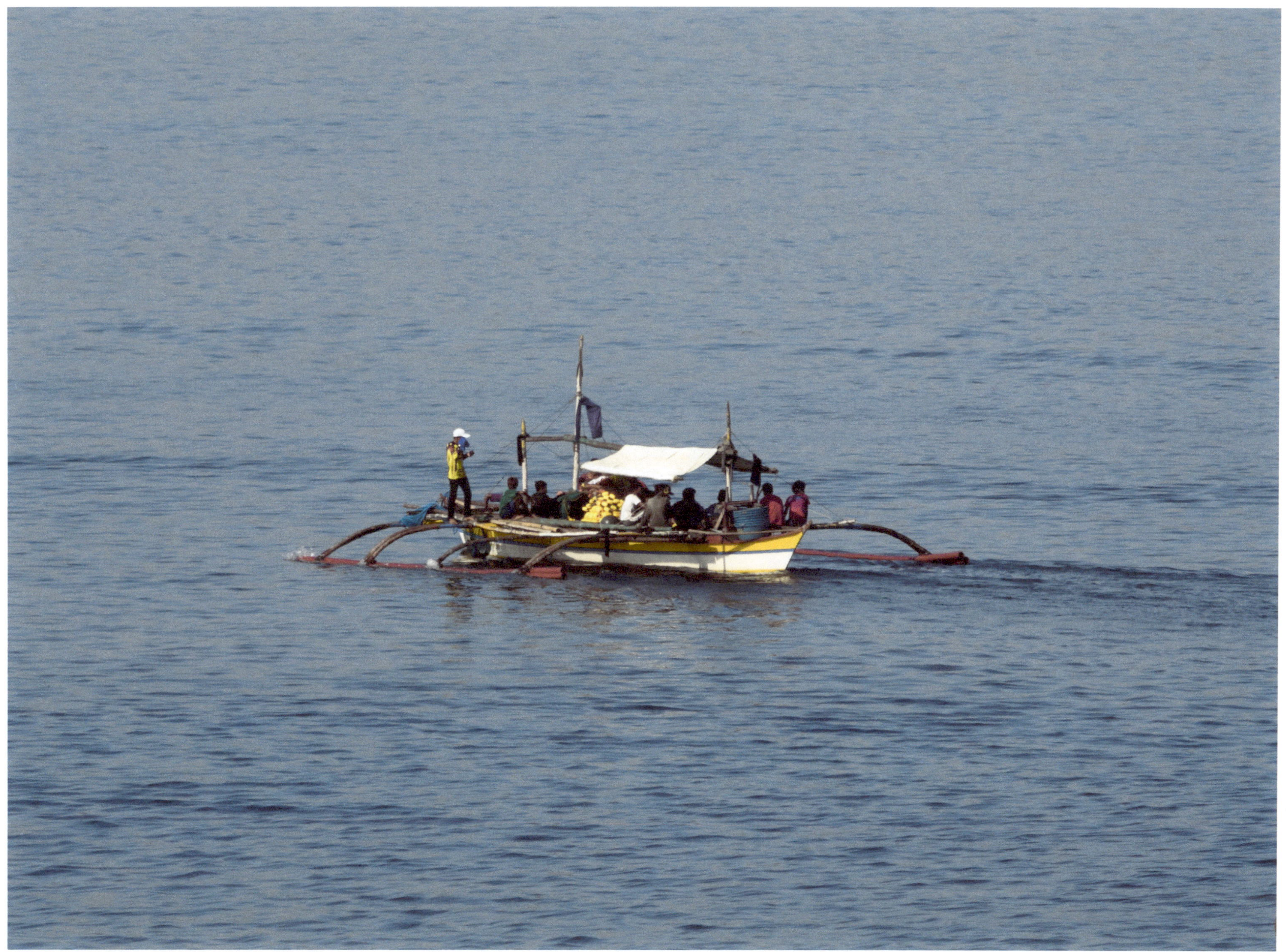

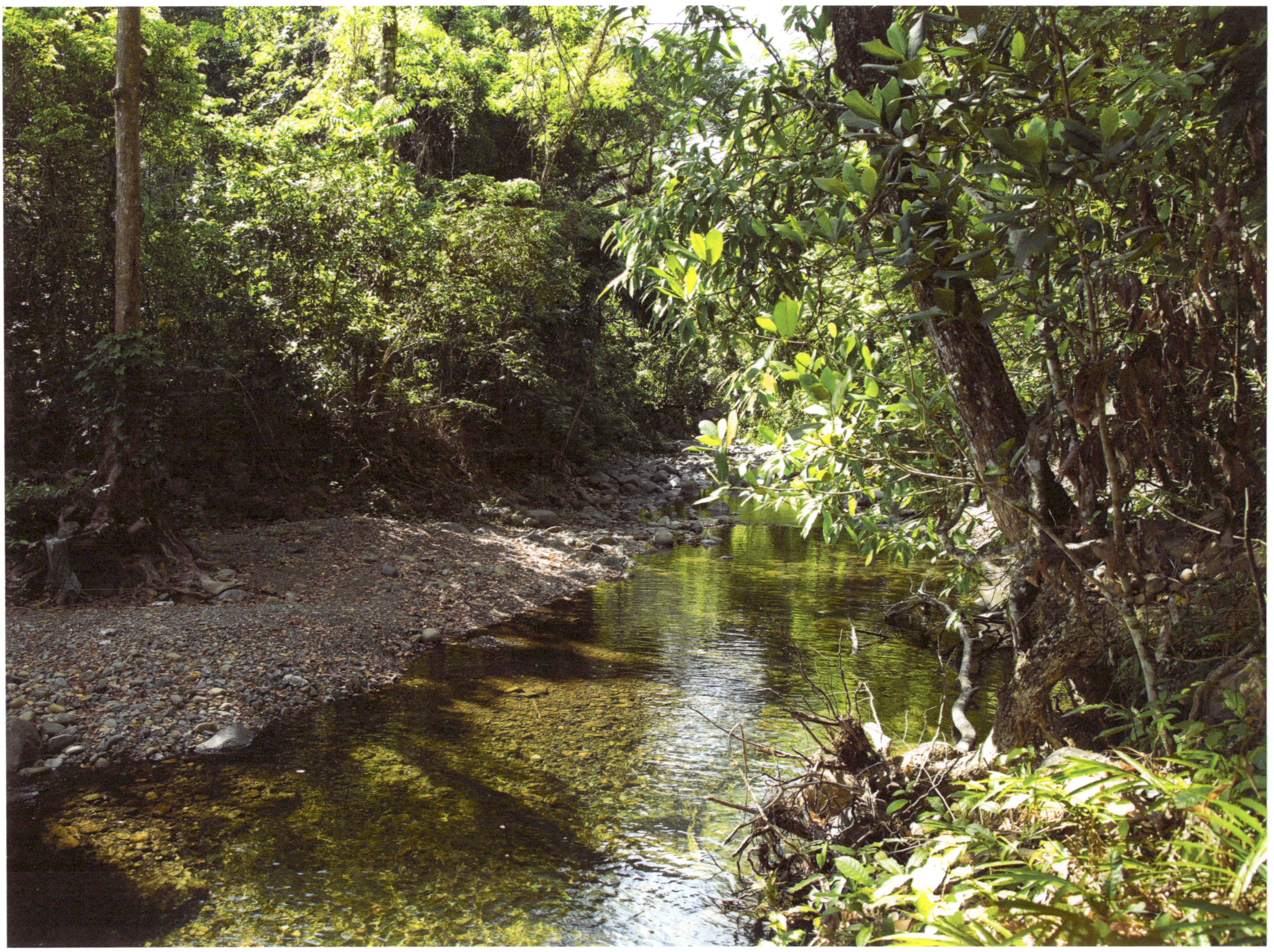

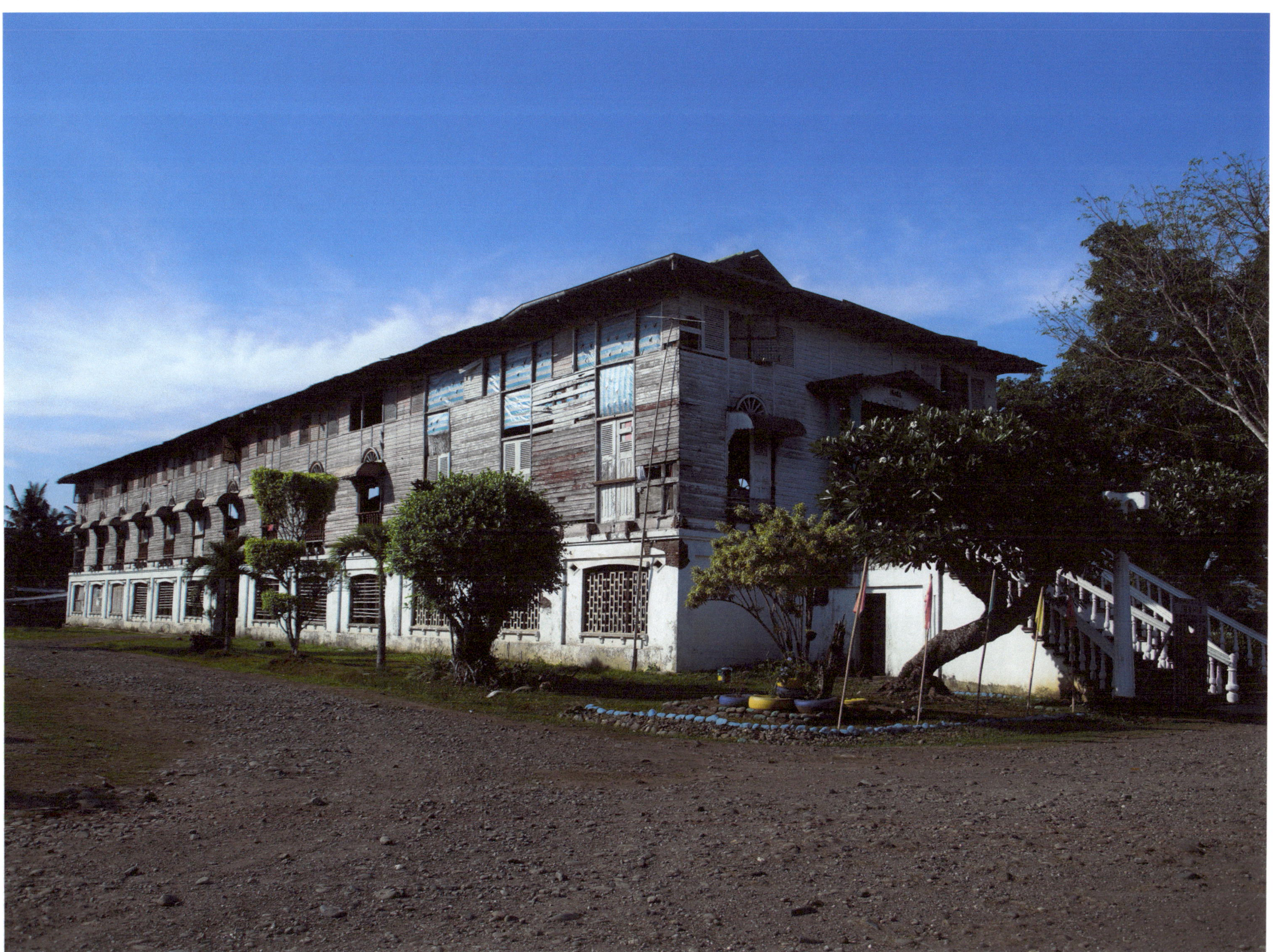

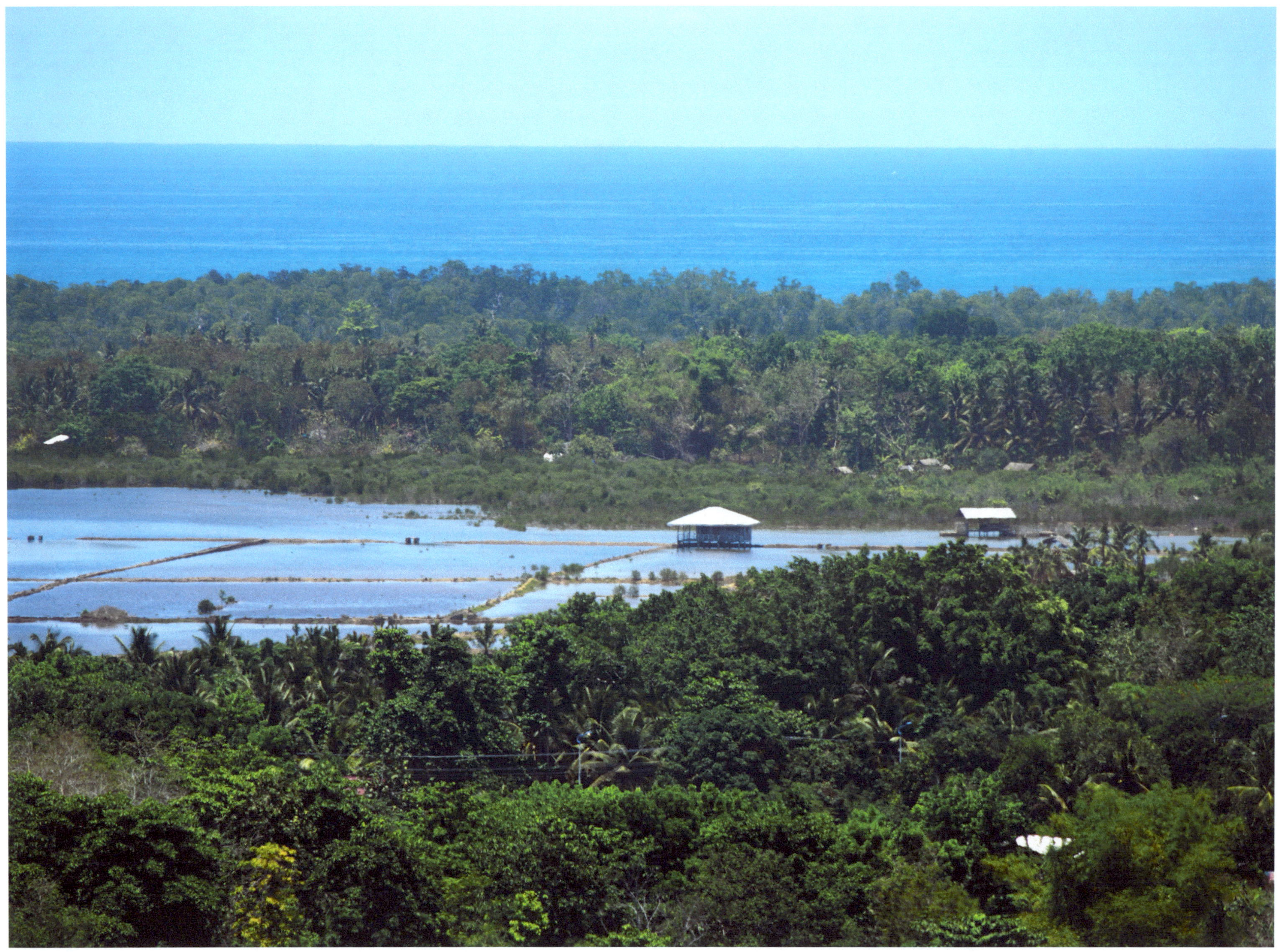

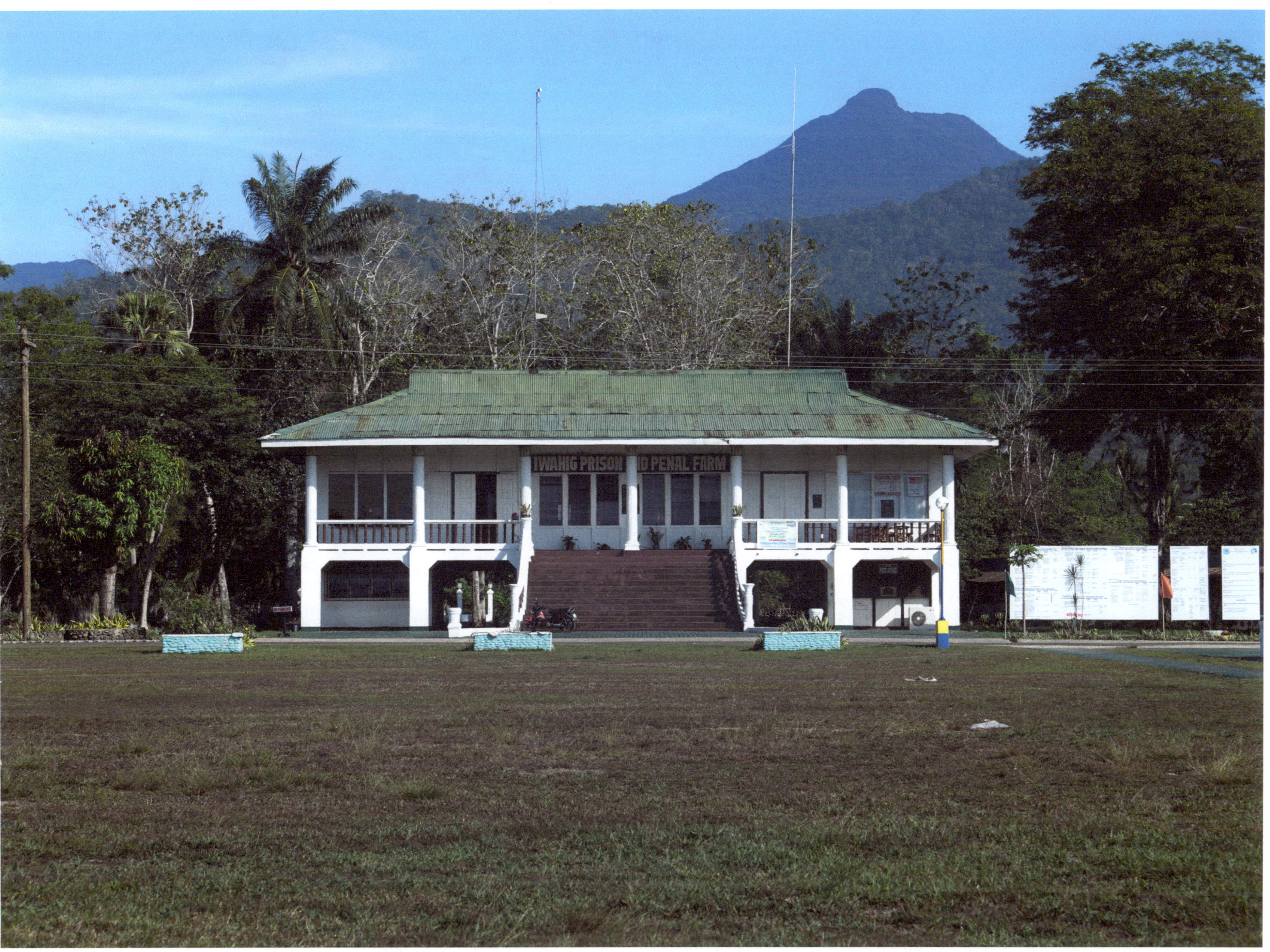
IWAHIG PRISON
D PENAL FARM

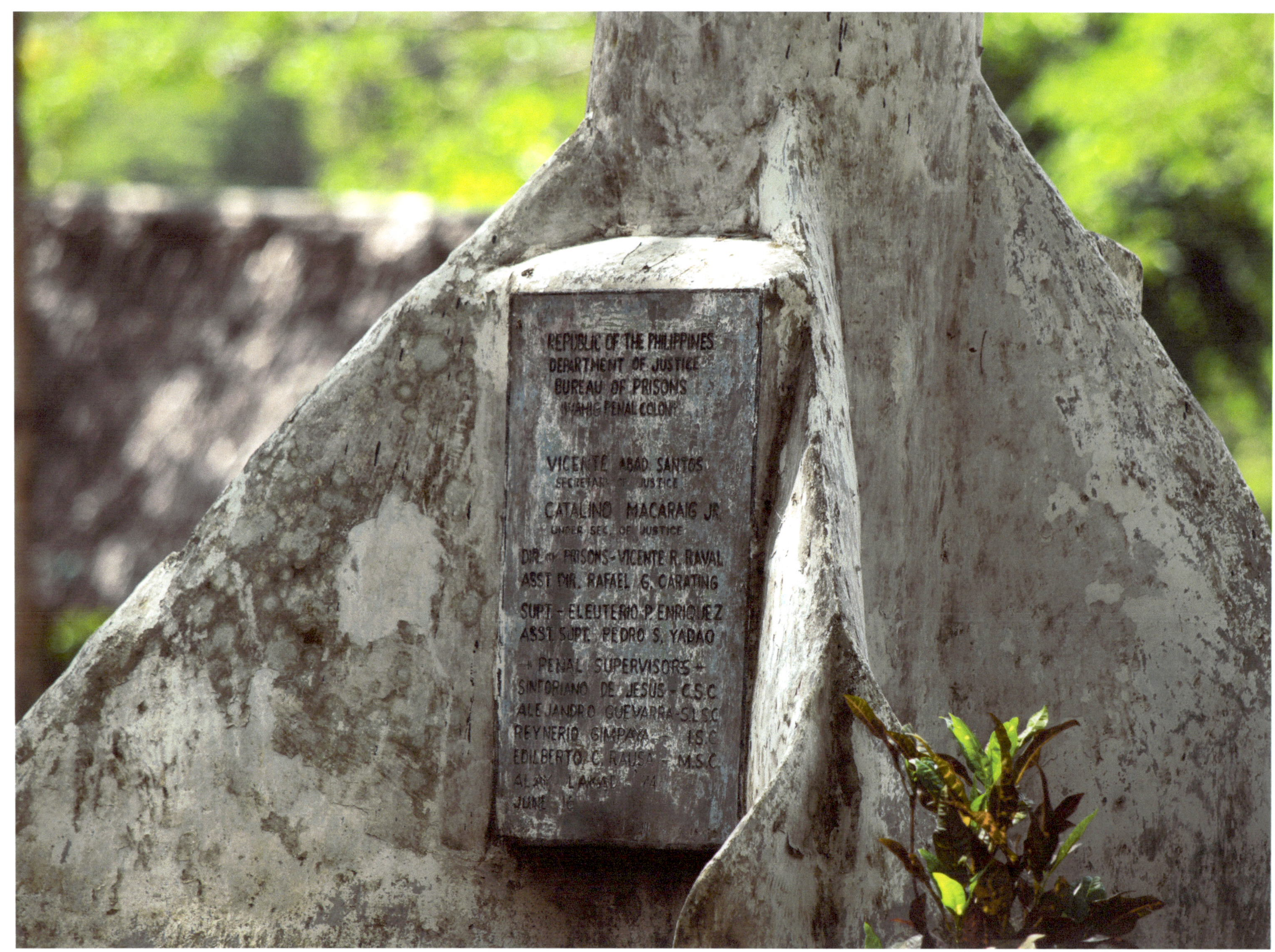
REPUBLIC OF THE PHILIPPINES
DEPARTMENT OF JUSTICE
BUREAU OF PRISONS
IWAHIG PENAL COLONY
VICENTE ABAD SANTOS
CATALINO MACARAIG JR.
UNDER SEC. OF JUSTICE
PRISONS - VICENTE R. RAVAL
ASST DIR. RAFAEL G. CARATING
SUPT - ELEUTERIO P. ENRIQUEZ
ASST. SUPT. PEDRO S. YADAO
PENAL SUPERVISORS
SINFORIANO DE JESUS - C.S.C
ALEJANDRO GUEVARRA - S.L.S.C
REYNERIO GIMPAYA - I.S.C
EDILBERTO C. RAUSA - M.S.C
JUNE 16

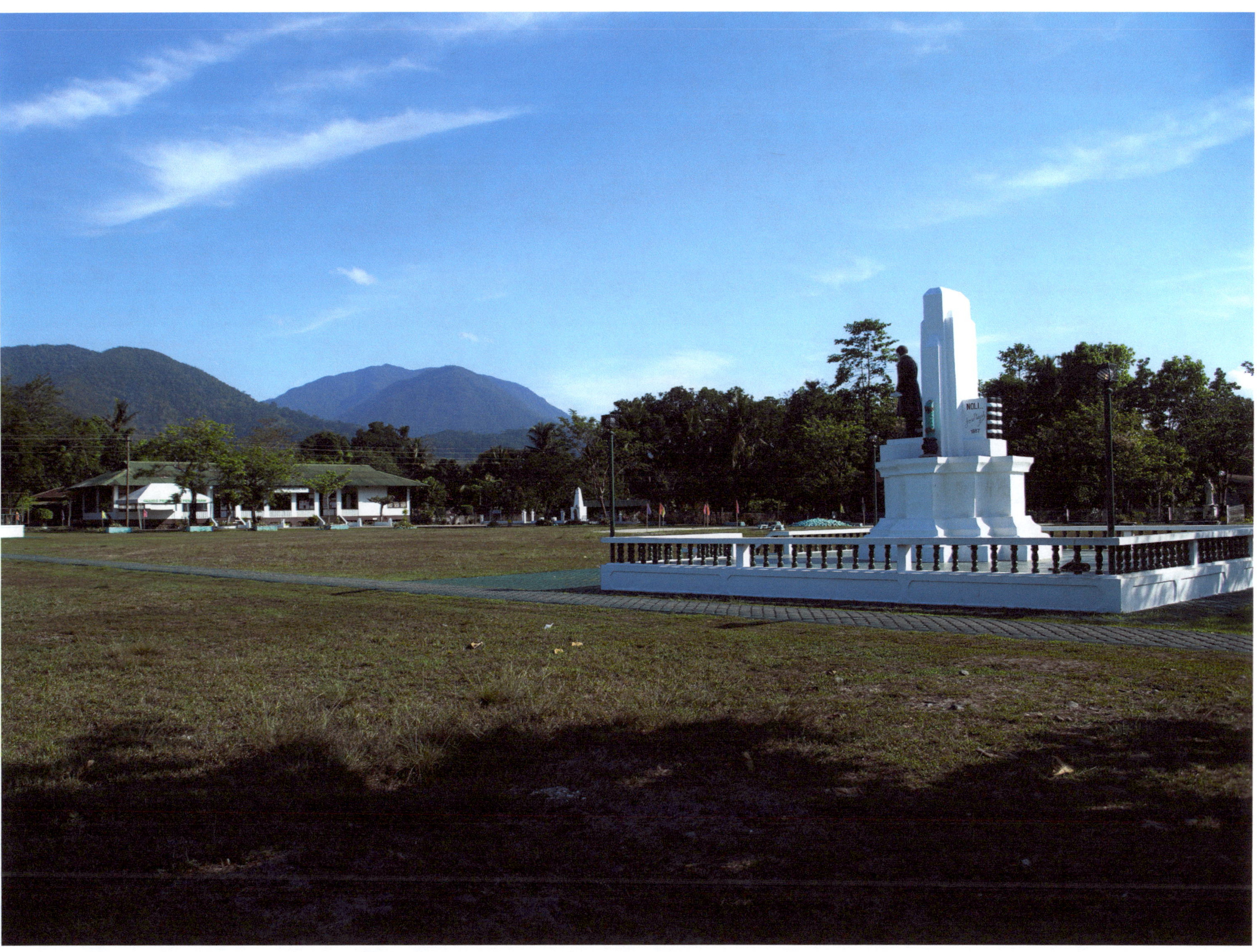
NOLI...

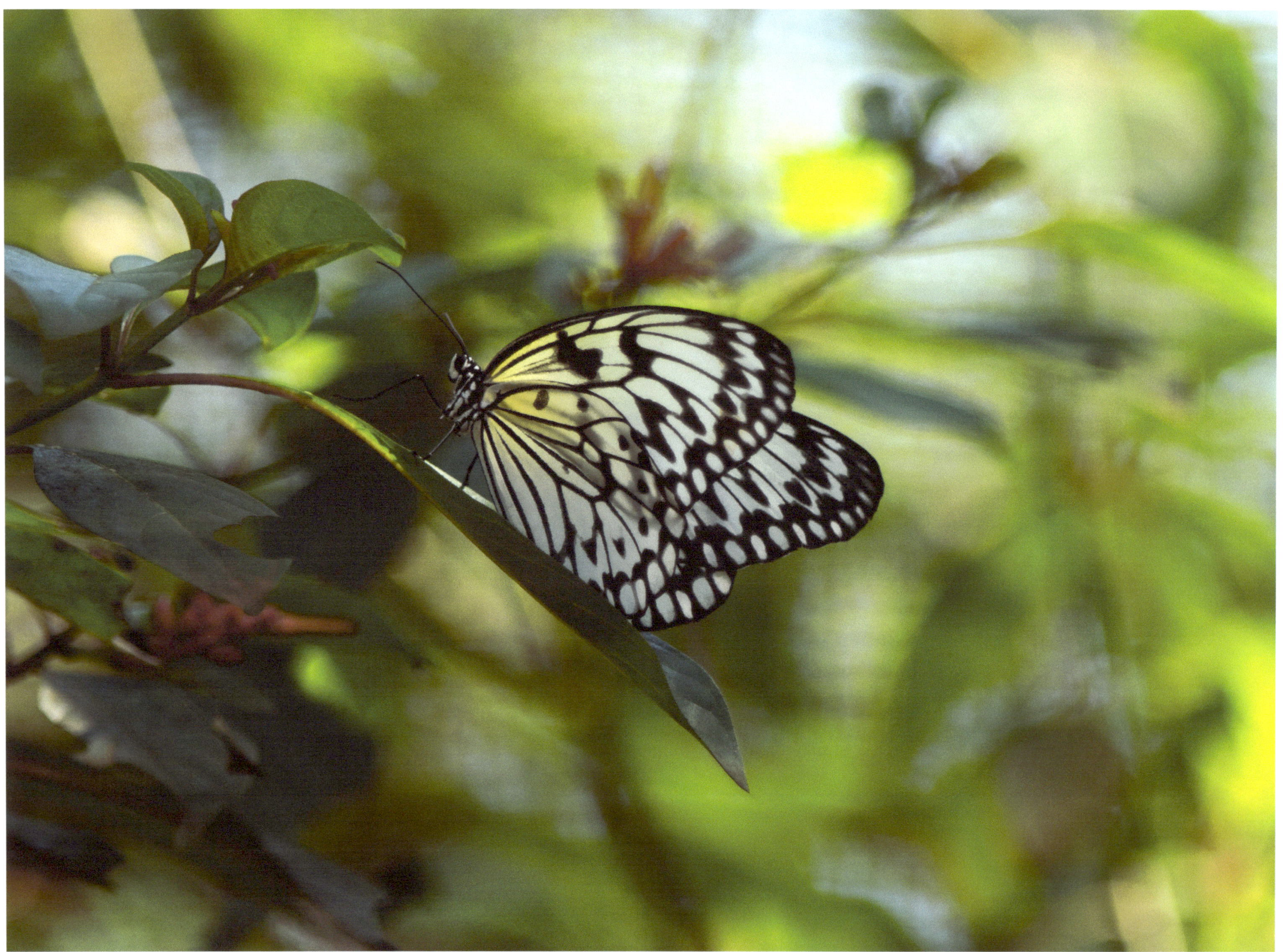

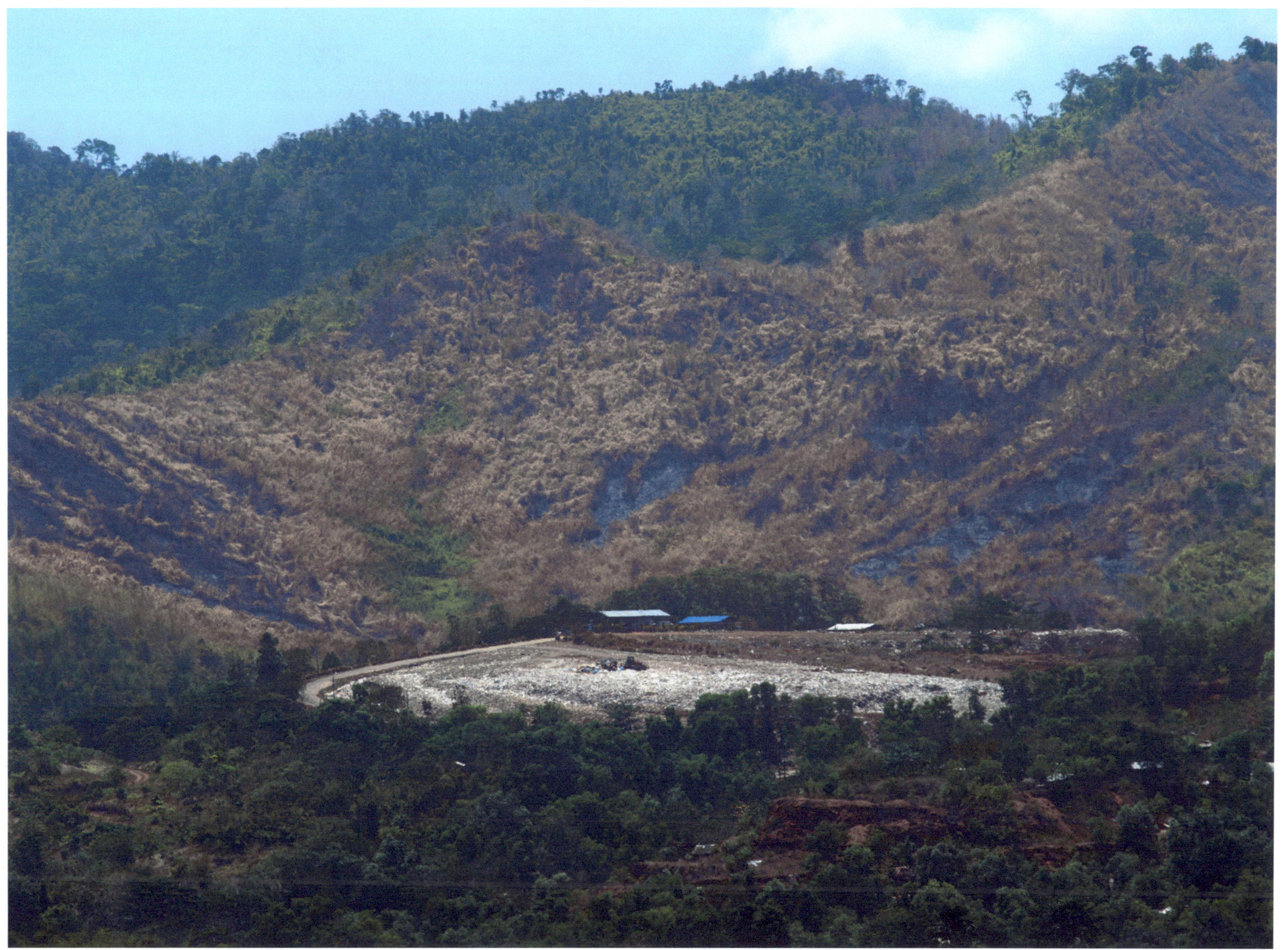

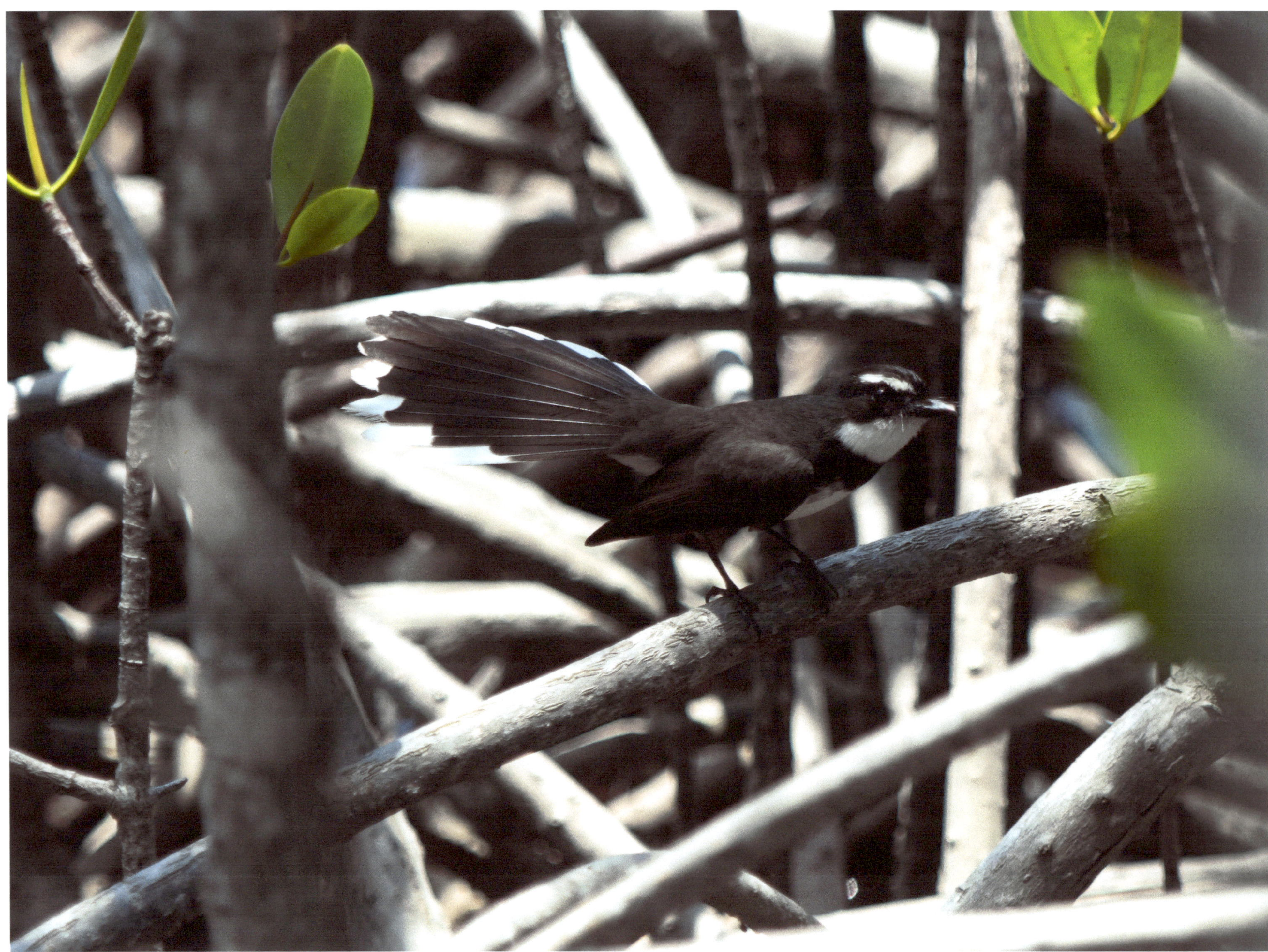

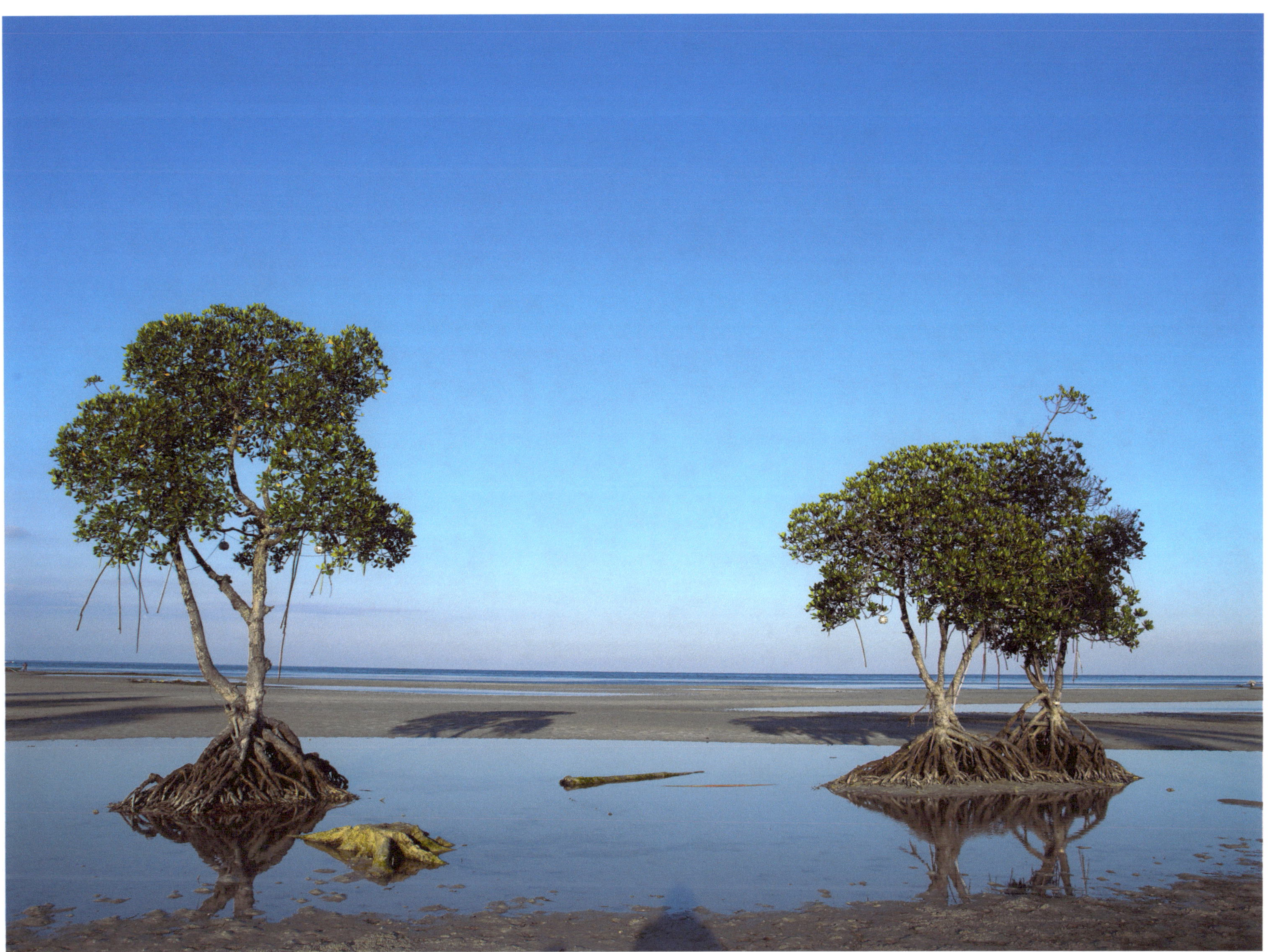

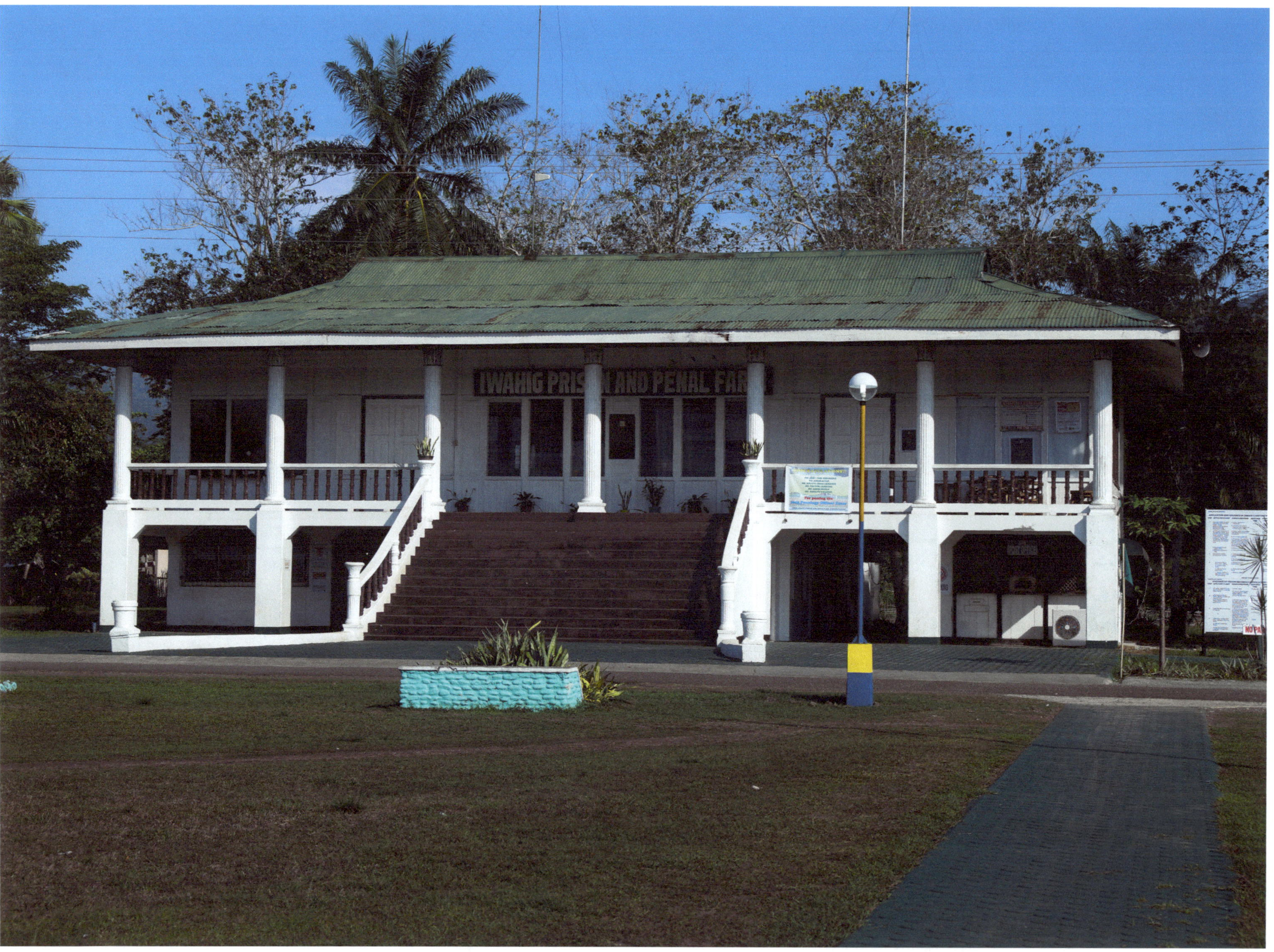
IWAHIG
AND PENAL

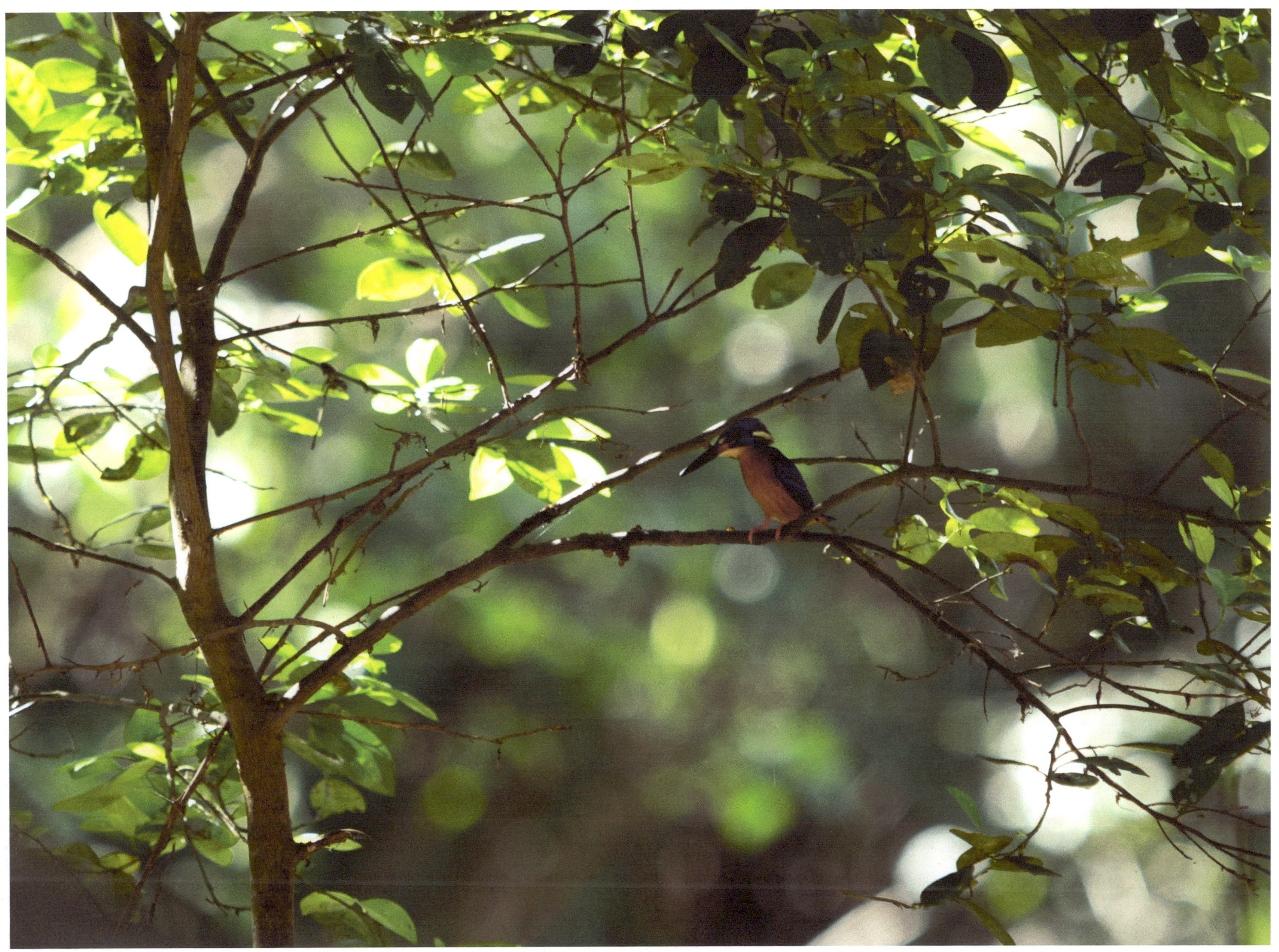

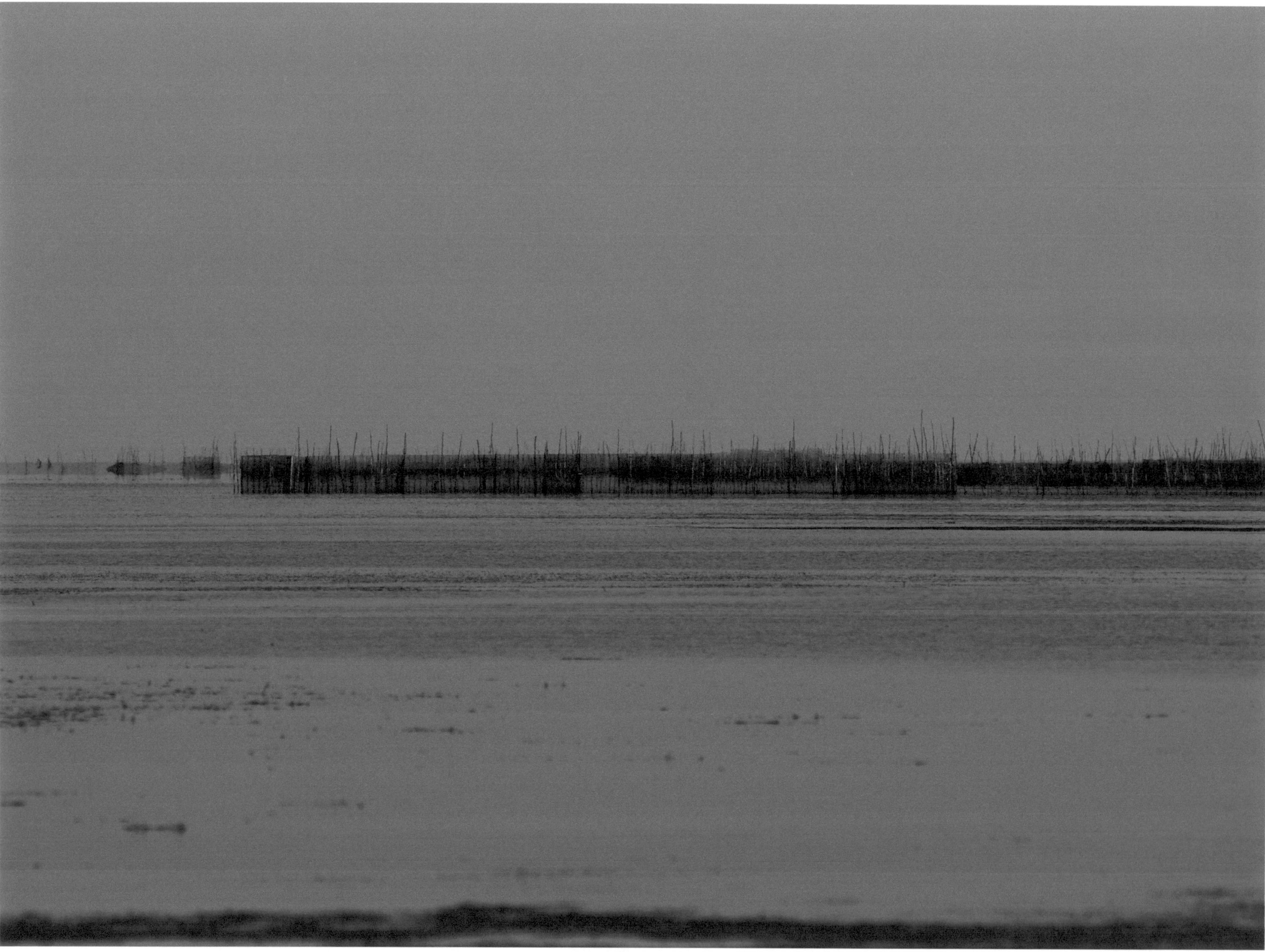

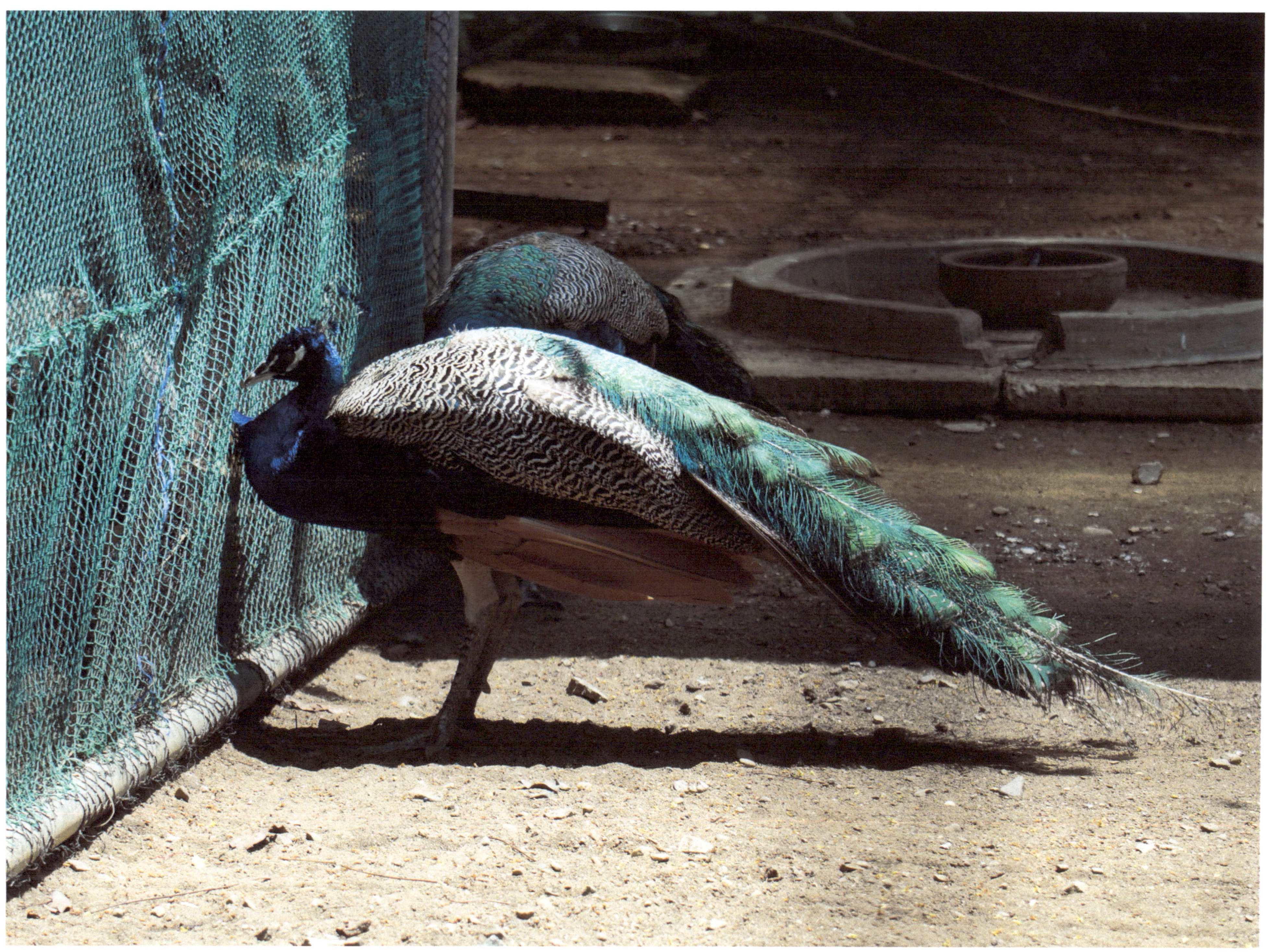

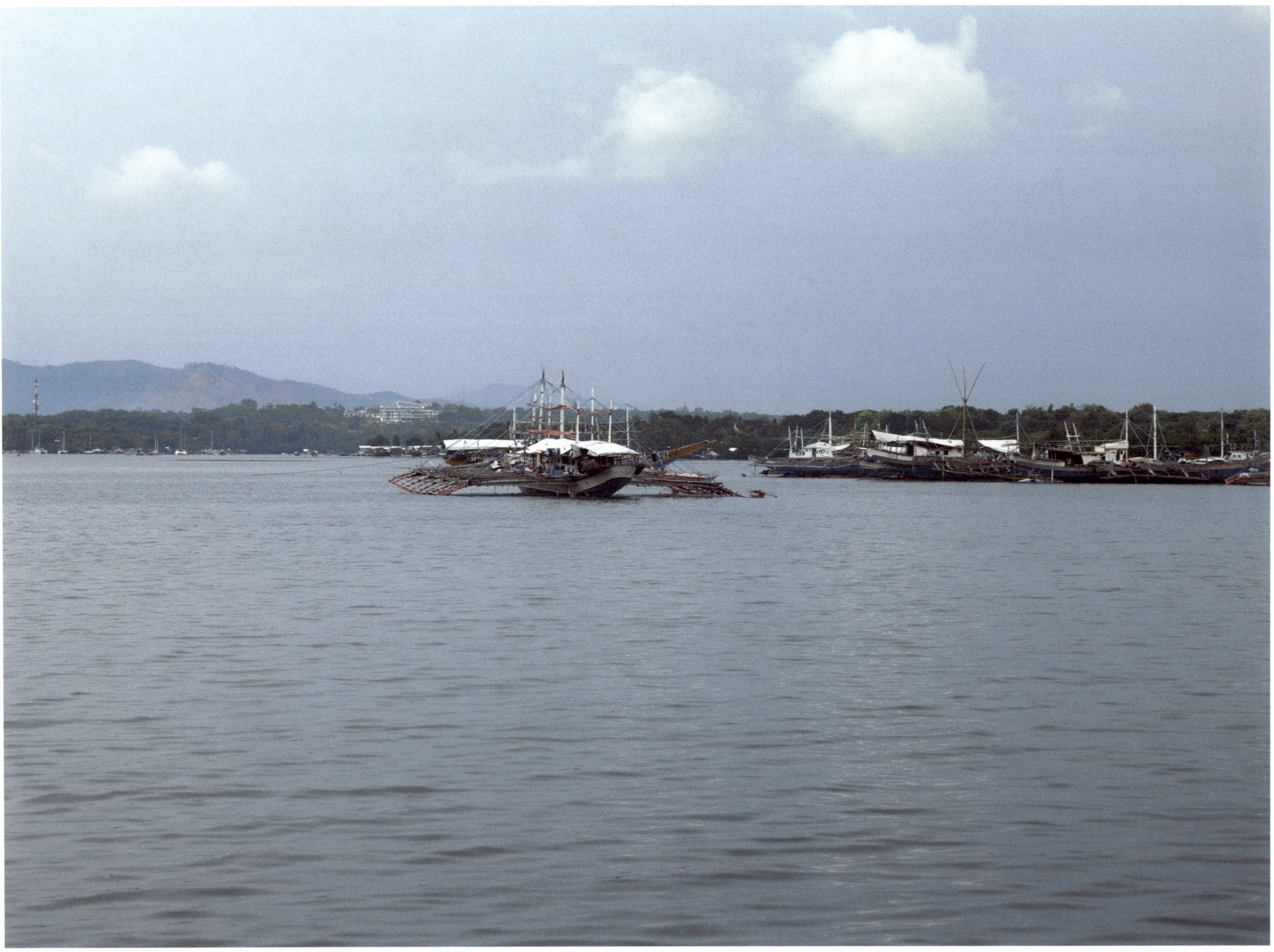

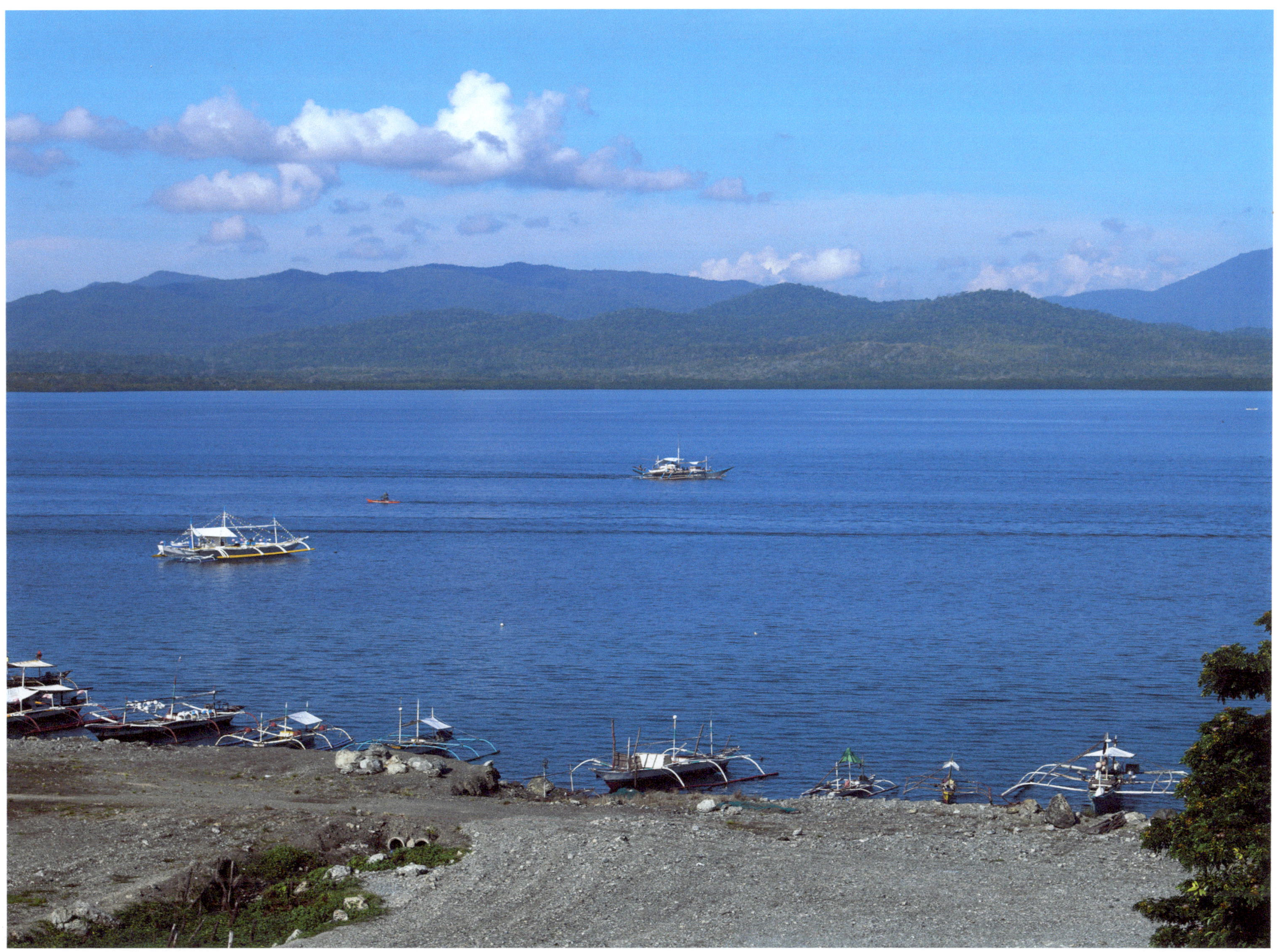

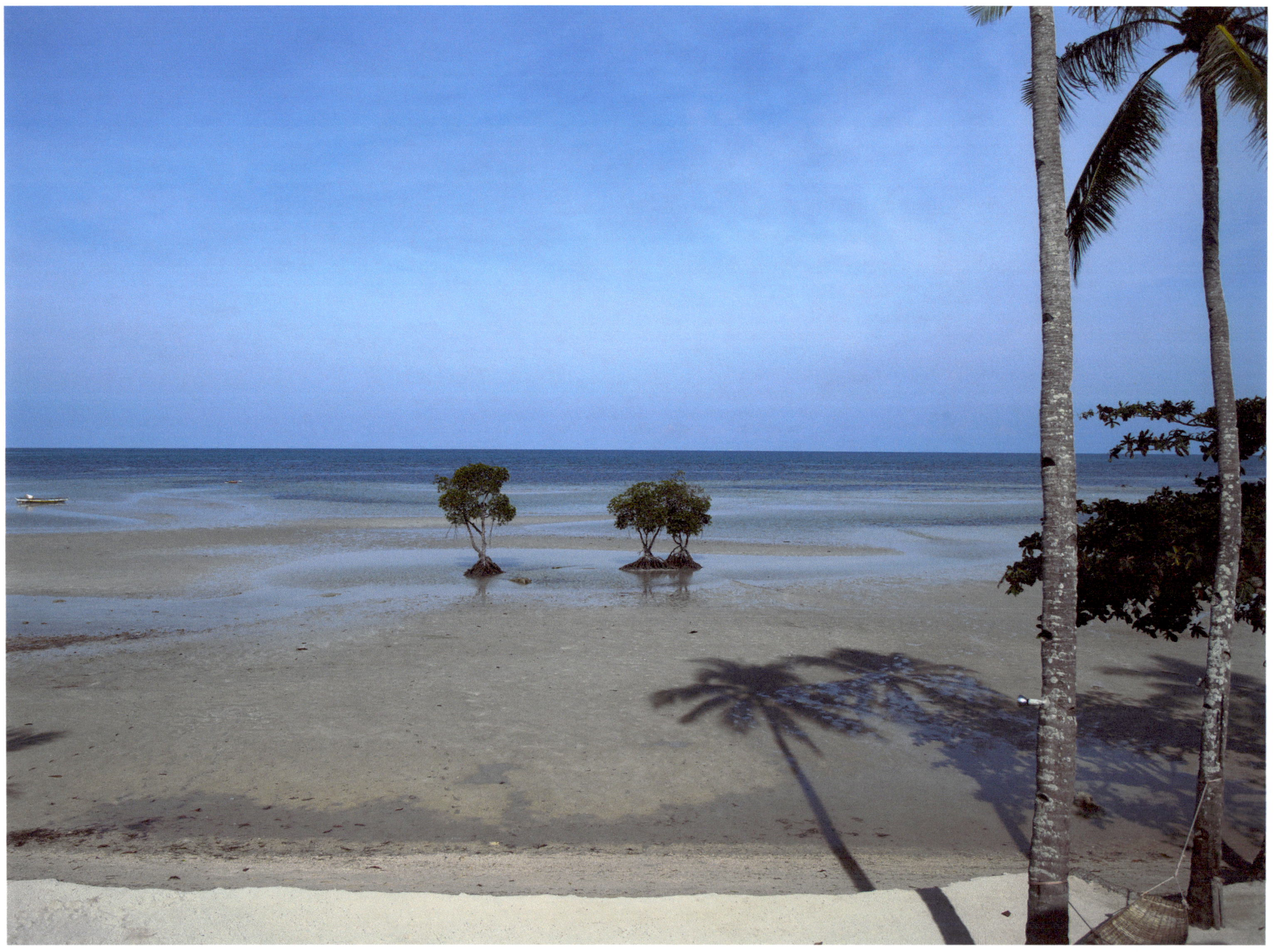

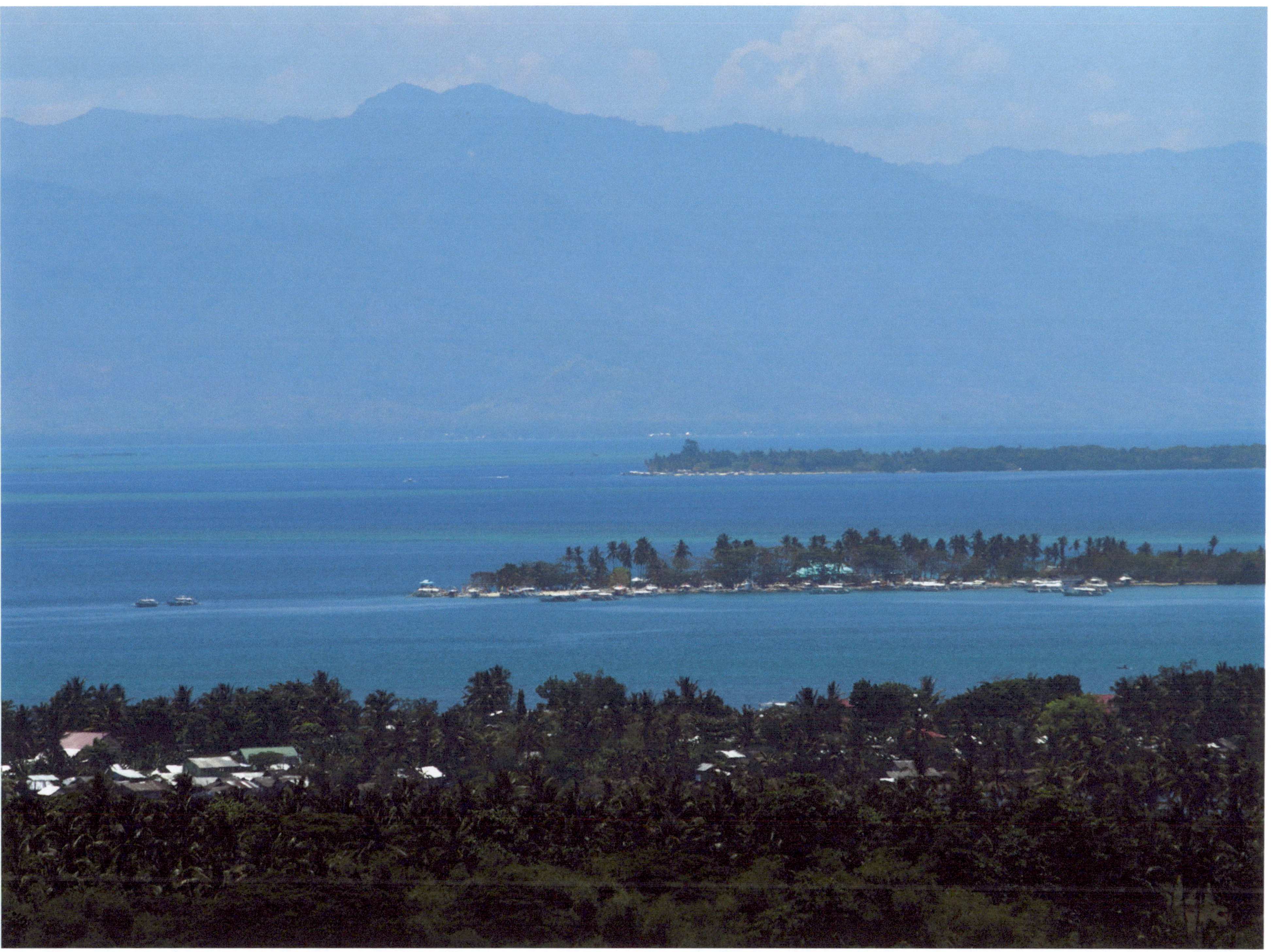

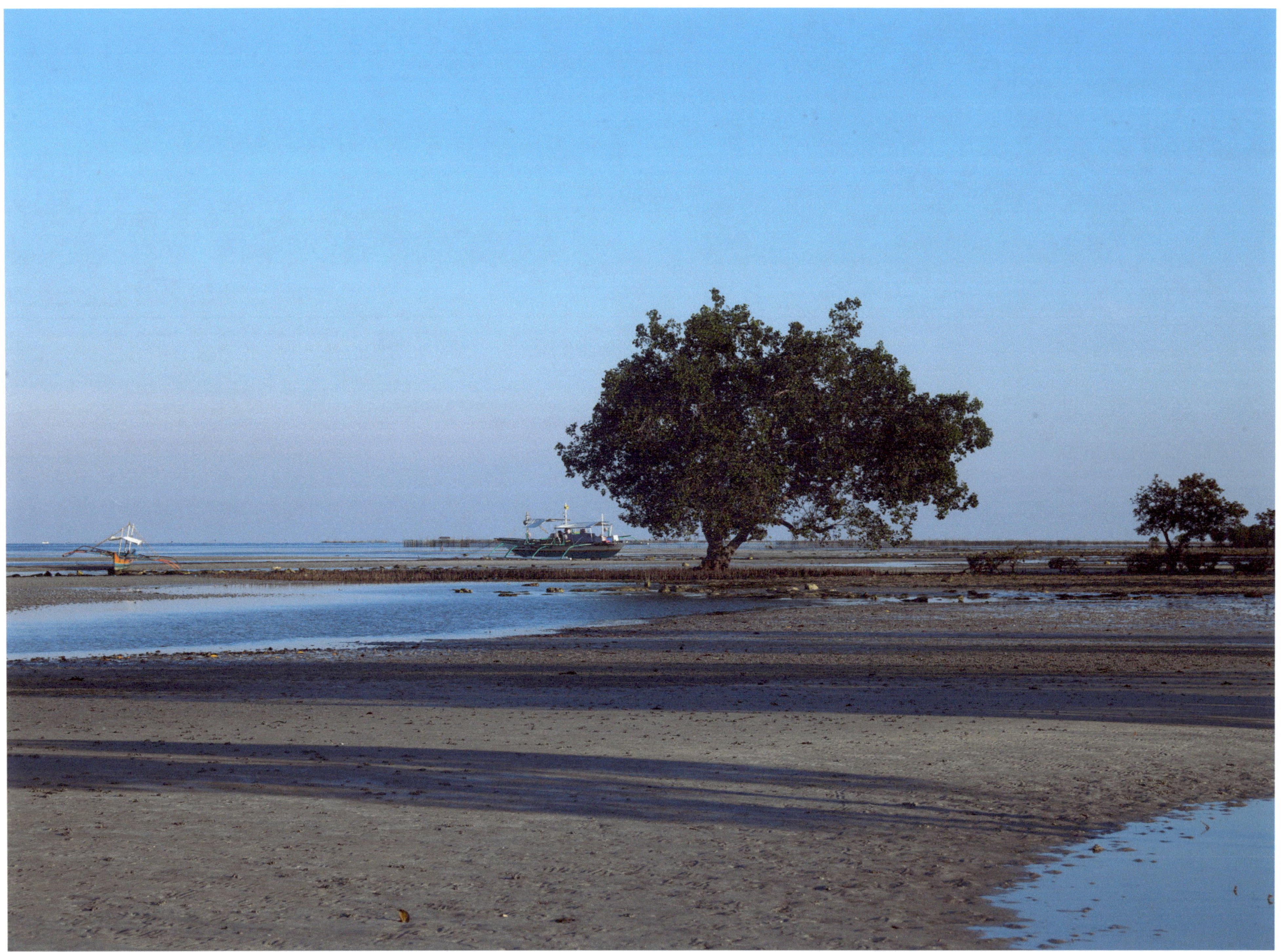

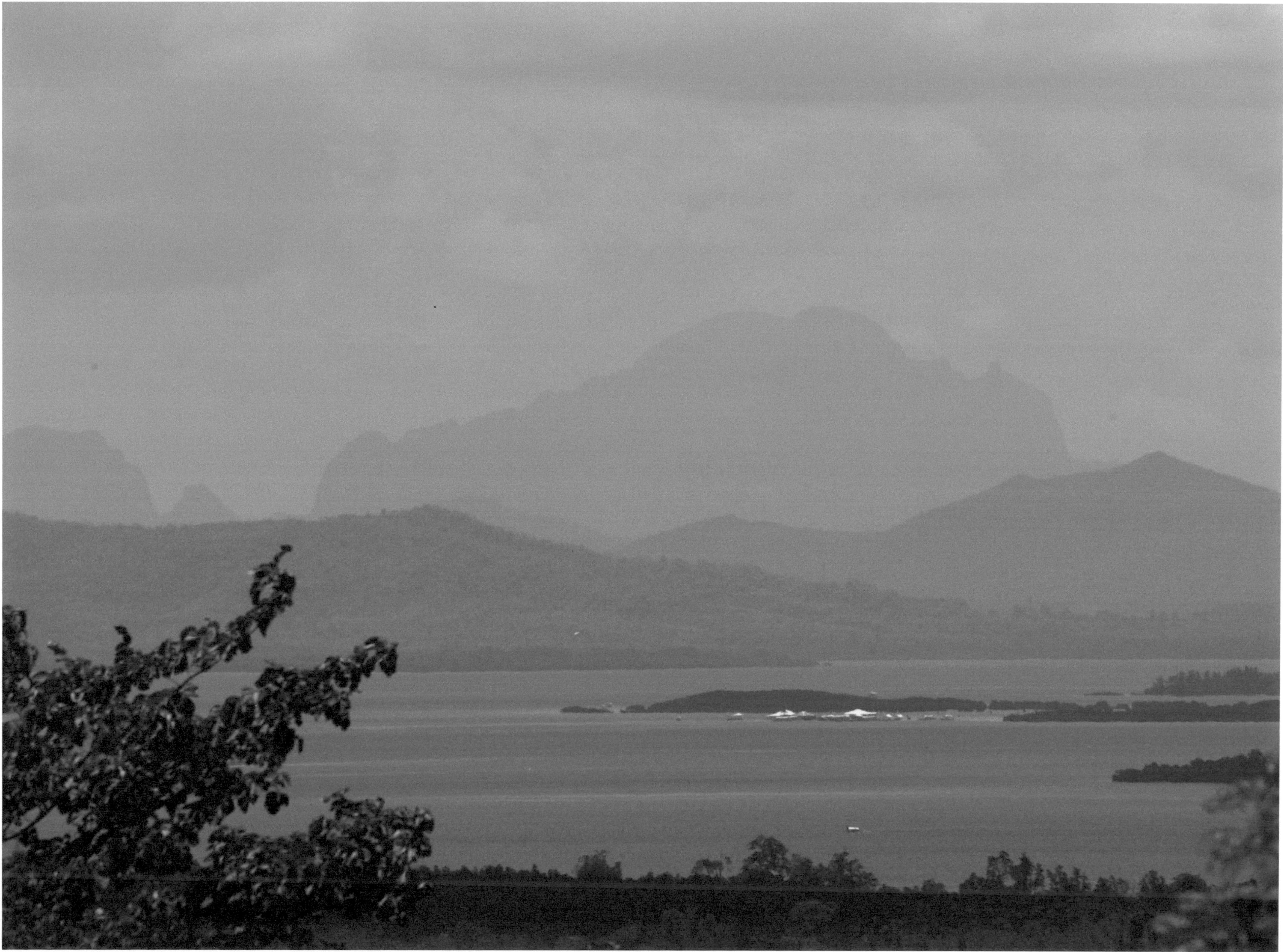

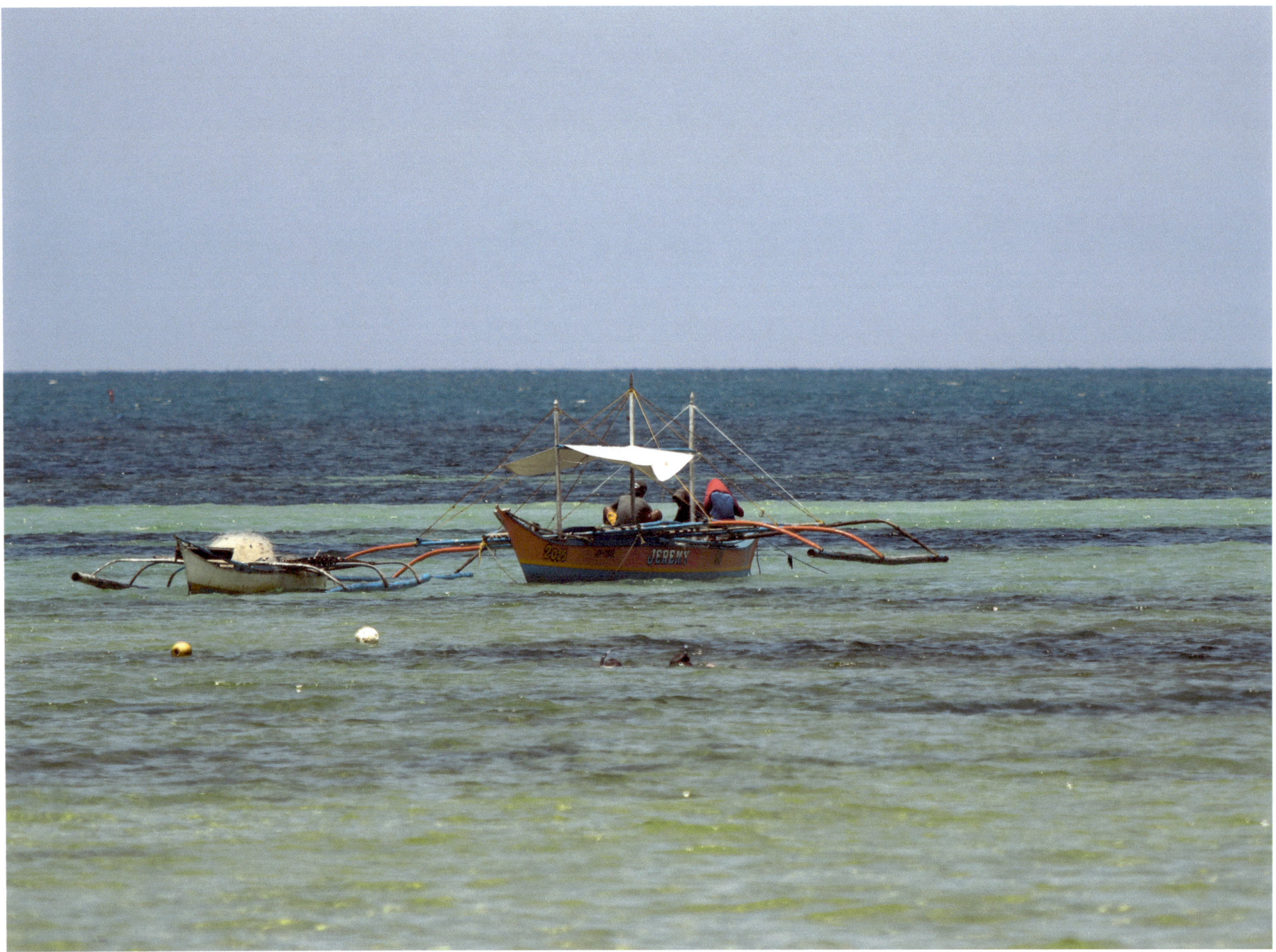
JEREMY

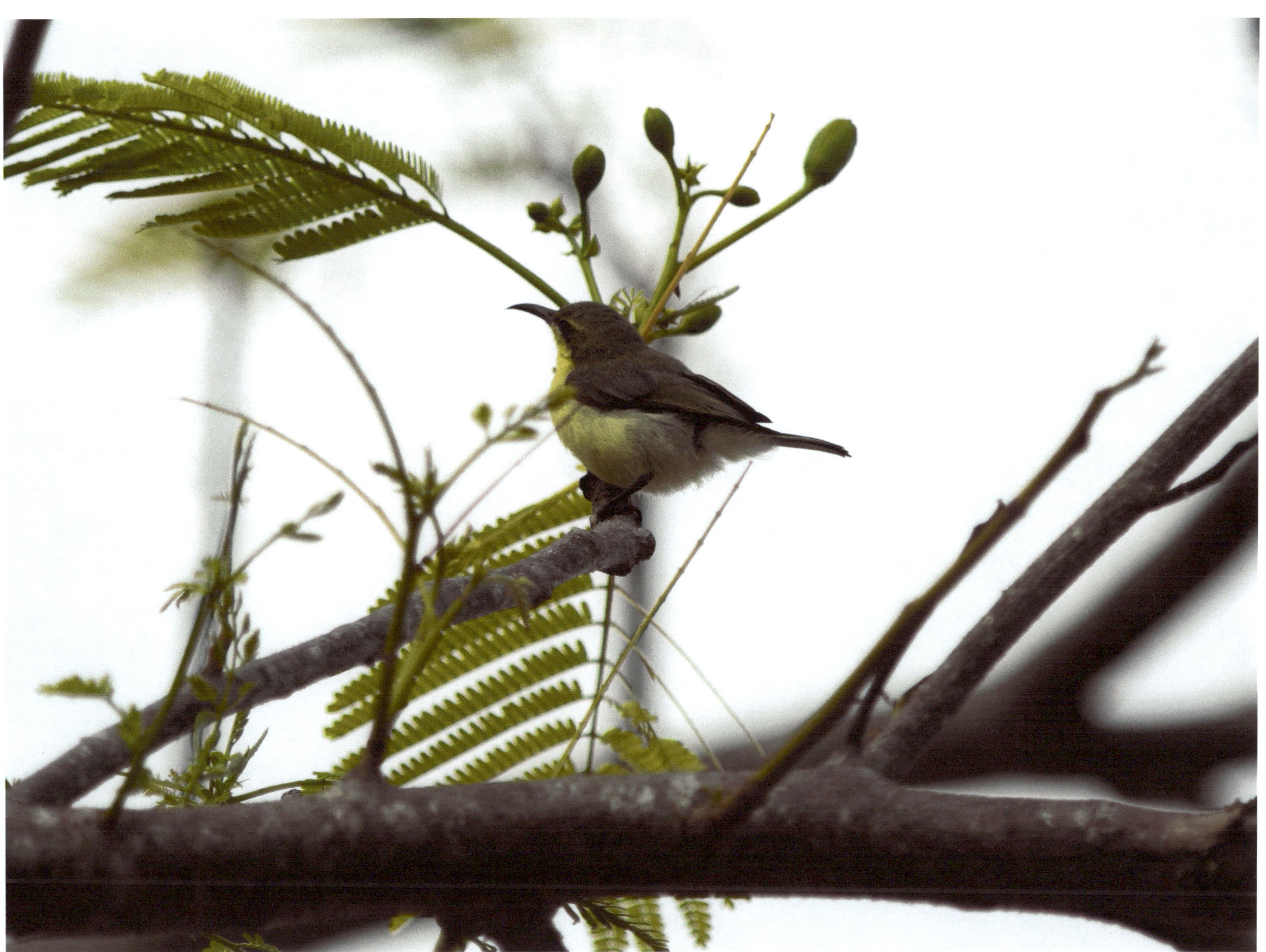

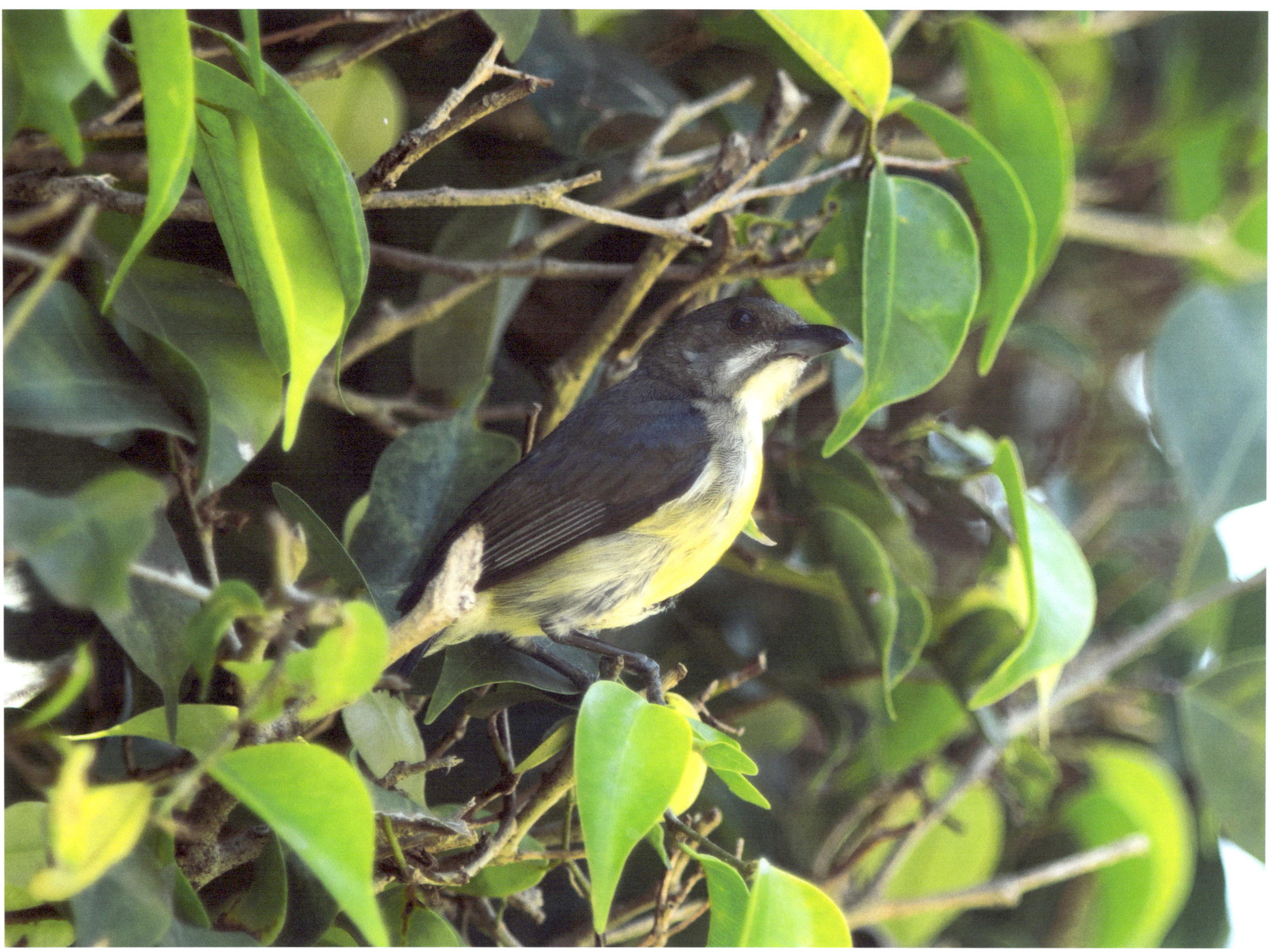

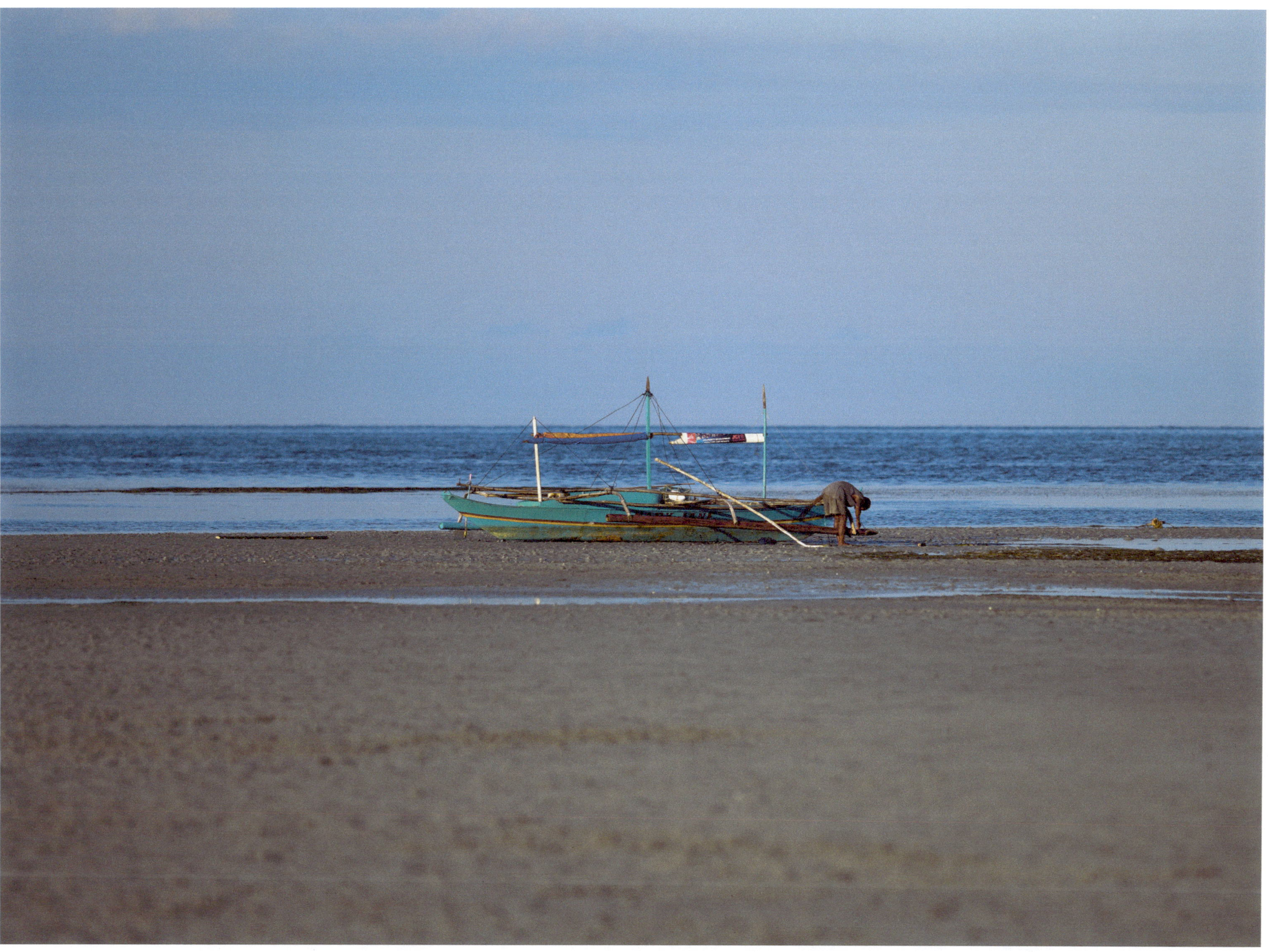

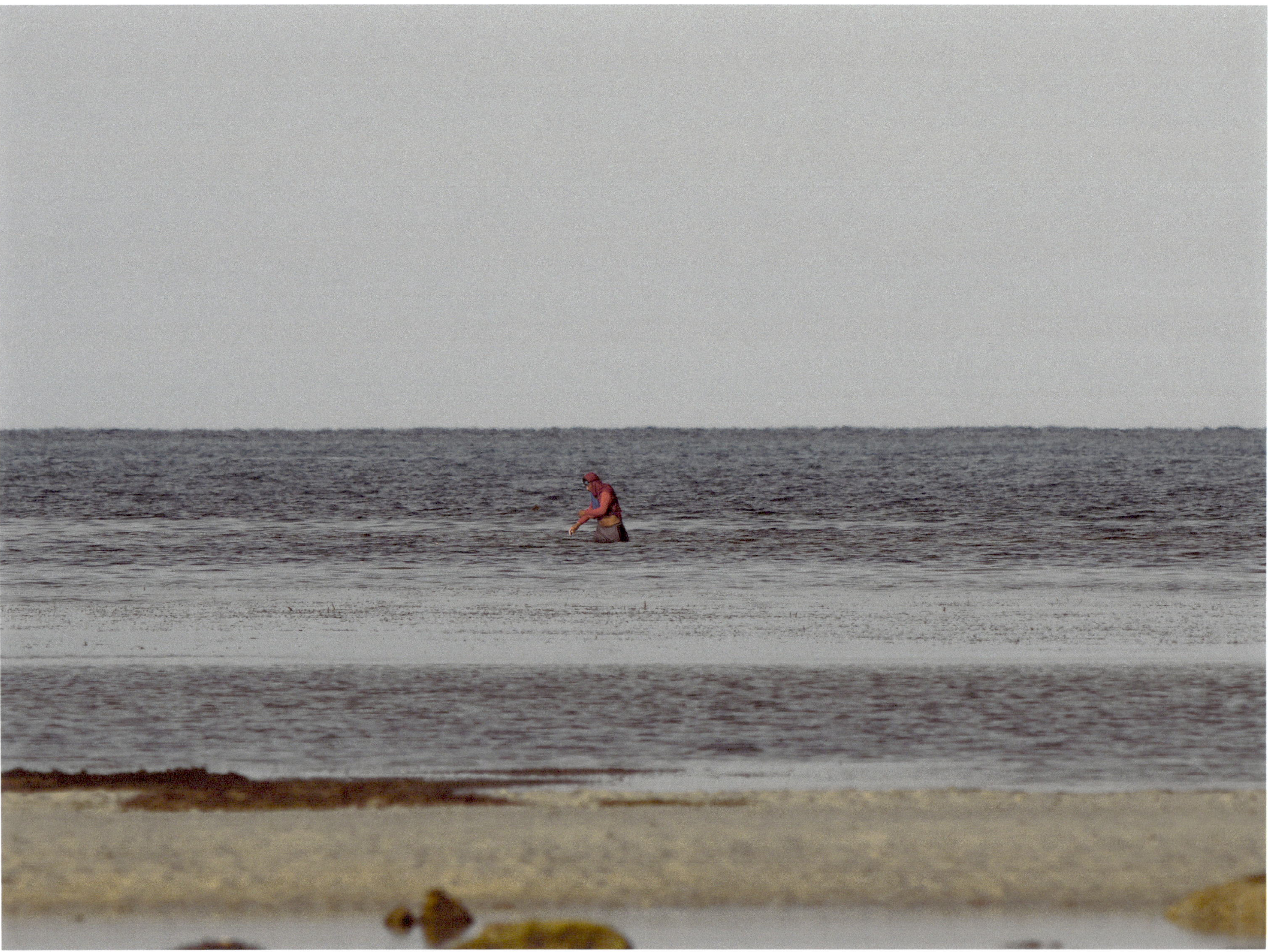

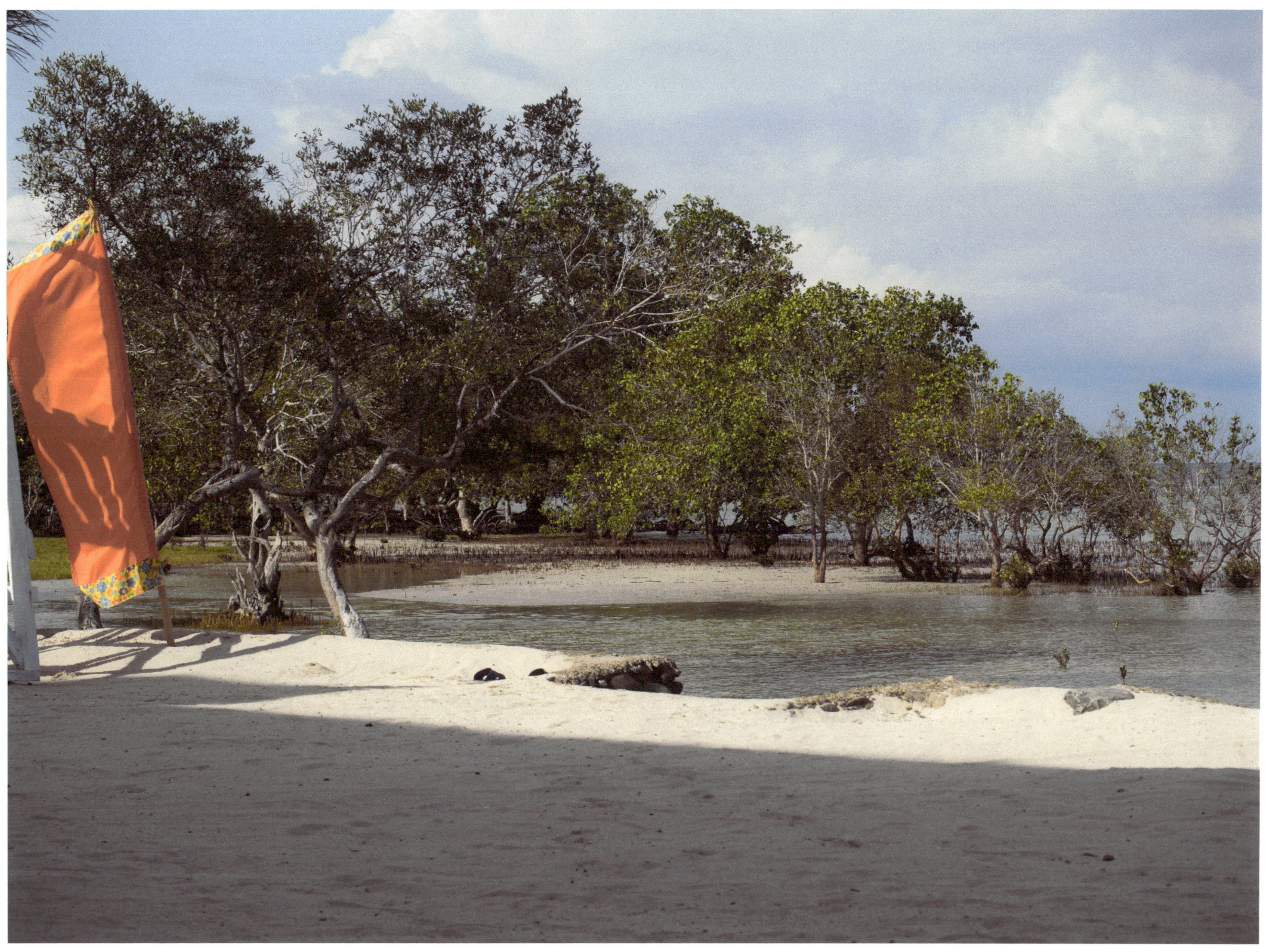

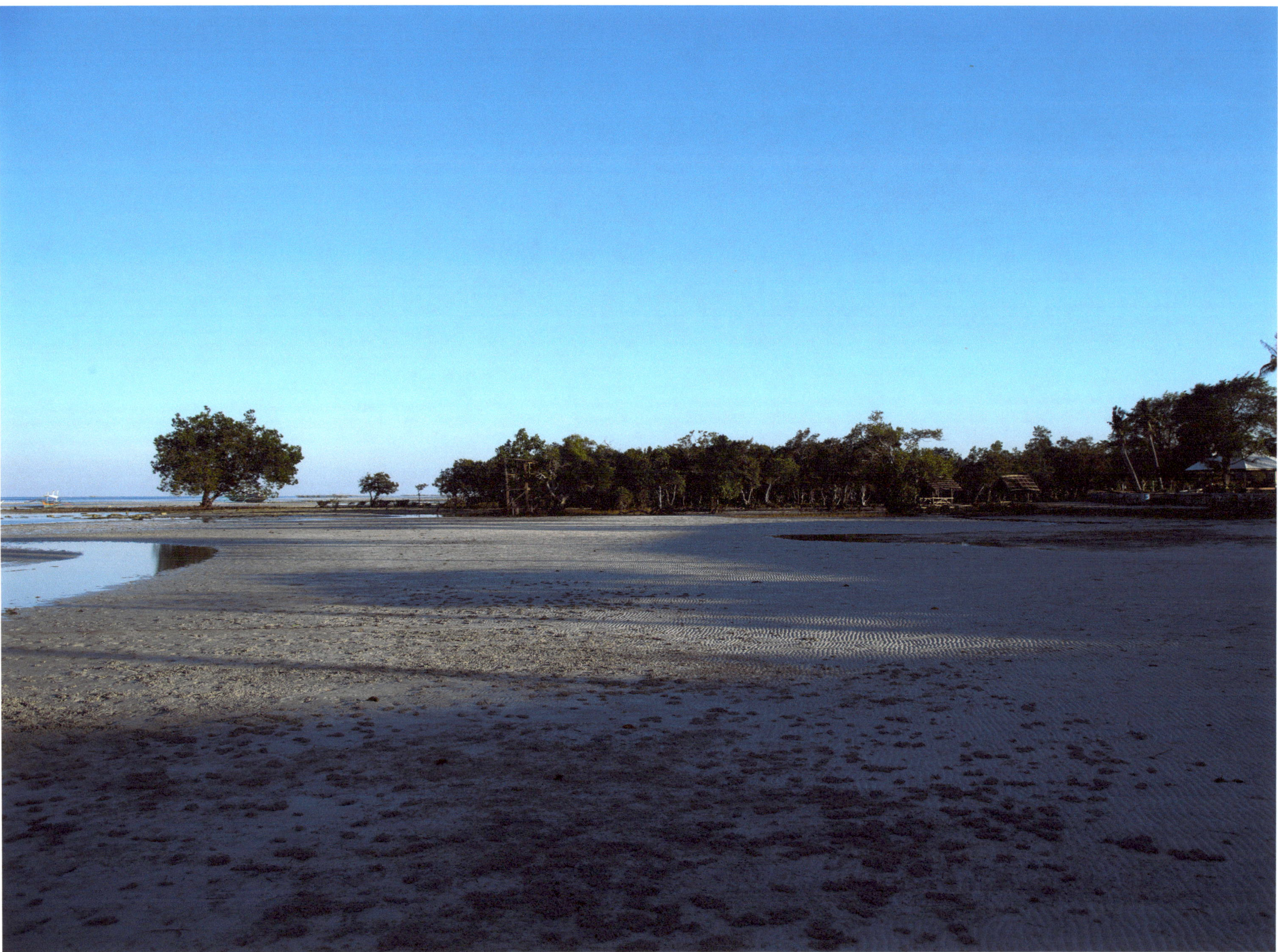

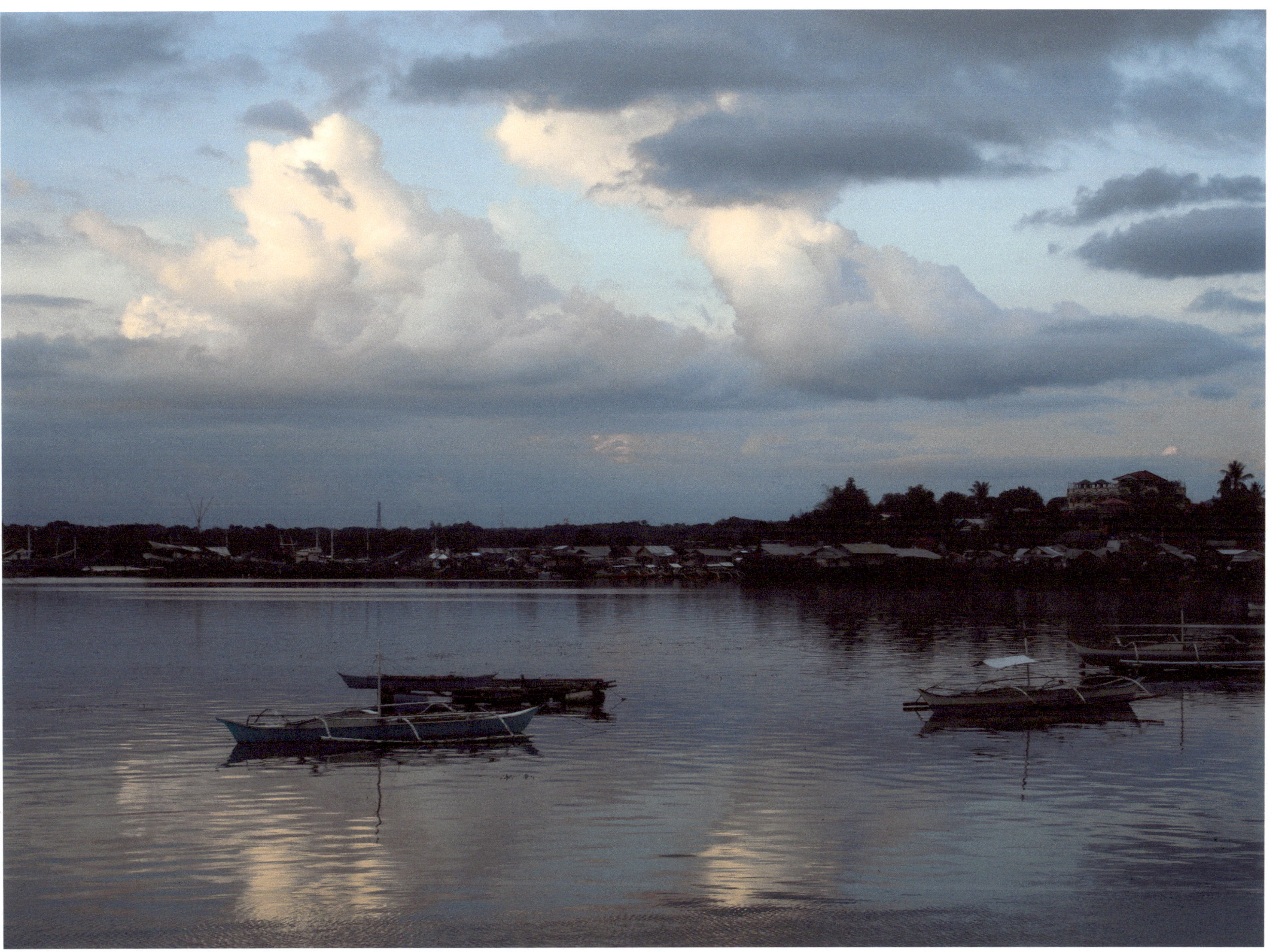

www.ingramcontent.com/pod-product-compliance
Lightning Source LLC
LaVergne TN
LVHW072330100826
845154LV00009B/147